SPIRITUAL PRIDE

We Are All Divine!

David Howard, PhD

PocketStone Publishing Powell, Ohio

Copyright © 2020 by David Howard

No portion of this book may be reproduced, translated, stored in a retrieval system, or transmitted in any form or by any means, electronic, mechanical, photocopying, microfilming, recording, or otherwise without written permission from the publisher.

Printed in the United States of America.

Editor: Hope Madden

Cover Design: David Howard

Interior Design and Layout: David Howard

Author Headshots: Jessica Lowman Photography

ISBN: 978-1-7341566-1-4

Important Note: The information provided in this book is designed to provide helpful information on the subjects discussed. This book is not meant to be used, nor should it be used, to diagnose or treat any medical or psychological condition. For diagnosis or treatment of any medical or psychological problem, consult your own physician. The publisher and author are not responsible for any specific health or psychological needs that may require medical supervision and are not liable for any damages or negative consequences from any treatment, action, application or preparation, to any person reading or following the information in this book. Our views and rights are the same: You are responsible for your own choices, actions, and results.

DEDICATION

This book is dedicated to the courageous gay men and women who, in the face of much adversity, fought for us to be seen and heard today. This book is also dedicated to the vibrant, inspirational and courageous gay men and women who today are following their hearts' desires and expressing their truths. Together we have formed a strong foundation for what it means to be gay—something to identify with and something to be proud of.

COVER ART

The colors of the front cover art depict the many representations of LGBTQ+ culture—colors found on the pride flag, the lesbian flag, the bisexual flag, the transgender flag and the pink triangle. The symbols are deconstructed to appear as strands flowing in an upward path—upward to symbolize our path of rising up. From a human perspective, the strands represent the many unique paths that LGBTQ+ people will take in our lives. We have the commonality of being part of the LGBTQ+ culture, but our experiences will be unique and sometimes quite different. On a spiritual level, the many colorful strands represent each of our unique Spirits that come together in unity to make up what I refer to in this book as our Spiritual Source—much more to come about that!

CONTENTS

DEFINITIONS USED IN THIS BOOK	1
WHY THIS BOOK NEEDED TO BE WRITTEN!	5
QUESTIONING REALITY	11
BORN THIS WAY: A SPIRITUAL EXPLANATION	19
OUR GAY JOURNEY	29
PERSONAL POWER	39
HEALING	49
THE HOLISTIC VIEW OF OURSELVES	65
BEING IN THE PRESENT MOMENT	79
AFFIRMATIONS	85
VIBES	91
THE LAW OF ATTRACTION	97
MANIFESTING	105
MEDITATION AND MINDFULNESS	113
INTUITION	123
CONNECTING TO SPIRITUAL SOURCE	131
THE AWAKENED GAY	143

DEFINITIONS USED IN THIS BOOK

Awakening- Coming to the realization that we are an eternal Spirit having a free-will human experience.

Ascension/ascending- A belief that we can transcend to higher realms of mind in our human lifetime.

Collective reality– an agreed upon reality held in the ego minds of a large number of people. It is based on what we collectively understand to be true, but does not mean it is actual truth.

Conscious mind- it's the mind that we are using to think in this moment. It is our mind that allows us to focus on learning, communicating, judging and analyzing.

Ego- An aspect of our conscious mind that leads us to describe, analyze and perceive our lives. Our egos are unique to each of us because they are a culmination of our cultural understanding, our education, and our life experiences. Our ego perceptions change and grow with us depending on our life experiences and learning.

Holistic- Seeing the whole of our human self as our mind, body and Spirit.

Intuition- Guidance that comes to us as an inner knowing or sensation/gut feeling. It comes to us from our Spirit and through the wisdom energies of Source—it is always in our greatest good.

Metaphysics- The spiritual and philosophical study of the higher eternal consciousness of our Spirit and how humans can benefit by expanding our awareness of it.

Personality- Our behaviors and mannerisms that we are born with and that will stay with us throughout our lifetime.

Raising one's vibration- We move into a state of higher vibration when we focus on positive thoughts and feelings.

Soul- Our Soul in this physical lifetime is the connection between us and our greater Spirit. Our Soul also connects us to the other energies that make up Spiritual Source.

Source- A word used to describe the force or energy that connects everything. It serves as the bond between each of our Spirits and it is also a source of knowledge. It is what some religions would refer to as God.

Spirit- The part of Source that chooses to have a physical experience. Our Spirit is expansive and exists in many realms simultaneously.

Spiritual Source- The non-physical energies that surround us all. Our spiritual home where our Spirit lives eternally. Heavenly realms. All that is. What religion would call God and heaven.

Subconscious mind- A repository of thoughts and feelings held within the brain and the cells of our body. It influences our health along with how we automatically respond to life events. It leads us to think automatic thoughts that we may consciously act on or not. It translates the energy around us into thoughts we can interpret—thus it allows for us to communicate with Spiritual Source.

Universe- When referred to in a spiritual context, it is a word used to describe when Spiritual Source takes action. Spiritual Source or the "universe" helps to manifest what we seek and works to bring balance to our personal energy and the energies around us. In a non-spiritual context, it's the place in which our world exists.

WHY THIS BOOK NEEDED TO BE WRITTEN!

Like many of us, I became exhausted with people using their religious beliefs as a reason to judge my gay lifestyle. When I was younger, I became so turned off by self-righteous and condemning ideologies that I wanted to have nothing to do with any type of belief at all, and for a period of time I didn't. But, regardless of the homophobic and demeaning speeches coming from political leaders, pastors on college lawns and religious zealots at pride parades, I felt my own connection to something great—something more beautiful and something divine.

I knew in my heart how I was created, and I knew that my sexual attraction to men and the love I later found with my husband were legitimate feelings coming from the core of who I am. This is what led me to overcome my disbelief, and it put me on a mission to seek wisdom, study spirituality and end up discovering that indeed there is a loving and accepting TRUTH to our gay existence. Because I am passionate about continuing to seek truth, my path led me to receive a ministerial Ph.D in metaphysical studies, author books and work with holistic coaching. And now, it is my greatest honor and passion to share what I have discovered with all of you!

Many of us have encountered negative experiences stemming from the followers of some religious beliefs, followers who use their own interpretations of scripture as ammunition to attack us and create laws to demean us. It's dismaying to encounter people who truly believe that hate and judgement are real aspects of God and heaven, especially when they refuse to see logic beyond what they believe themselves. Because of people using religion as a basis to attack and judge gays, who can blame any of us for losing interest in pursuing a spiritual path—no one wants to believe in something that condemns who they are. However, it's very unfortunate that by dismissing the idea of a spiritual belief altogether, we will miss out on discovering a loving and accepting truth that actually does support us—a truth that has historically been shrouded by dogma and pushed aside by the people who scream judgement and condemnation.

Beyond the fire and brimstone religious preaching, there lies a true spiritual reality that consists of a loving and supportive Spiritual Source that is always here for us—all of us. Why is it ALWAYS here for us? Because this Spiritual Source is part of who we truly are, and it is also our eternal home. The problem is, most of us do not know how to discover that it exists, and even if we do, most of us will not understand how to create a beneficial connection to it. This became the inspiration for me to write this book—to put confusion aside and help others become aware of our greater spiritual reality. This book will show you that there is a real Spiritual Source to our existence and how we can connect with it; this Spiritual Source wants nothing more than to support our human experience. Further, this Spiritual Source wants all gay people to know: you are beautifully created; you are on an amazing spiritual journey; you are eternally loved; and you are

Why This Book Needed to Be Written!

always part of a beautiful spiritual reality. There, someone finally told you the truth!

For those of us who are already on a spiritual path, it's likely we recognize how spirituality is a journey of growth and the process of mentally opening our minds; it is something that grows with us. When I began seeking spiritual truths, I was thrilled to eventually come across beliefs that were supportive and accepting of my being gay, but as I continued to evolve in my spiritual understanding, I began to see some of the limitations of these beliefs, too. One of the greatest limitations is that the beliefs I encountered still implied there is a God who thinks with a human mind and because of this, it is judging us. This type of thought leads us to believe that we must be more "pure" in our actions to reach out to God or to be able to go home to a heavenly realm. As for being "pure," many of the spiritual beliefs that I have encountered suggested that to be on a spiritual path we must be vegan or vegetarian, we must meditate, be alcohol free, be willing to fast, be pacifists, be against sexually explicit material, be in a committed relationship or be willing to give up wanting material things. But, these beliefs were merely reflecting the current attitudes and preferences of the spiritual people who promoted them.

Finding accepting beliefs is a stepping stone to opening our minds and hearts to spirituality, but our spiritual paths will all be unique—we are all different in what we like and dislike. Thus, it is fine to be on a spiritual path and not like things such as alcohol, meat and sexually explicit material but it is also just as fine to be spiritual and enjoy these things. Also, some of us on a spiritual path may choose to meditate, give up materialism or fast to enhance our spiritual experience, but these are not essential choices—it's all personal choice. I will explain in this book why all of these preferences are just part of the human free will experience. It is only our own human minds that are determining what is right or wrong or good or bad. There is not an ultimate being in heaven judging us for indulging in human activities. Humans are the

Spiritual Pride

only ones doing the judging.

I do not believe: that we are here to release spiritual karma that carries from one lifetime to another; that we come here to be put to a test to accomplish a spiritual mission; or that we are here to try and reach some sort of ascension to get back to an ultimate level of God. Yet, if these are beliefs you wish to hold onto, there is nothing wrong with that. We should follow the path that we are most comfortable with. So, as you read this book, please be open-minded, there is no one size fits all when it comes to having a belief. Having spiritual pride means recognizing that we are all unique in our physical, mental and spiritual needs.

In the chapters ahead, I will discuss in-depth ways to heal our minds and bodies along with holistic concepts such as manifestation, intuition, spiritual alignment, and how the energy of our own thoughts and feelings influences our life experiences. I will also discuss the journey of being gay from a spiritual perspective, along with some of the reasons why our Spirit chooses to have a gay life experience—it's all beautiful, it's all divine! How we each choose to interpret the energy of Spiritual Source is up to each of us and just part of our individual human experience, but I will wrap up this book by teaching techniques for connecting and aligning ourselves with our Spiritual Source. We are having a free-will experience on Earth, so for this book, I do not add hierarchies, expectations, rules or any other requirement to following a spiritual or holistic path. I believe these concepts just add complicated layers that lead to overthinking spiritual truths. Spirituality at its core is simple: we come here to experience being human, and how we view this journey is ultimately up to each of us as individuals—we have free will to perceive as we choose.

This book is a journey to help you find pride in having a spiritual belief, a belief that compliments and nourishes your gay reality and experiences. This book will lead you to feel empowered as a gay person because I will show you that you are here to express yourself in

Why This Book Needed to Be Written!

a joyful and loving way; you are beautifully made, and your feelings and desires are completely valid! I hope this book brings you comfort, wisdom and joy, but most of all I hope it inspires you to express your heart's desire, be who it is you want to be in this lifetime and if you choose, have pride in being spiritual about it!

> *"The spiritual journey is individual, highly personal. It can't be organized or regulated. It isn't true that everyone should follow one path. Listen to your own truth."*
> *—Ram Dass*

QUESTIONING REALITY

Each of us has our own personal reality based on our beliefs, experiences and what we have learned in our lifetimes. The thoughts that reflect our own reality—such as our judgments and opinions, along with how we analyze and come to conclusions—are called our ego thoughts. We each have an individual ego mind, our unique way of thinking that influences how we perceive our own reality and the world around us. It's through our ego thoughts that we describe our beliefs about life, and it's our ego mind that we use to stereotype or judge other people.

Humans who think similar ego thoughts will form a collective reality, which is an agreed upon reality held in the minds of a large number of people. Collective realities include ideas such as religious beliefs, judicial laws, beliefs in the power structure of the countries we live in and concepts we learn through our general educations. Yes, it is an agreed upon reality held by a large number of people, but this does not make these ideas universal truth. If a person finds themselves easily fitting into and being accepted by the majority collective reality, then they are likely to accept their collectively held beliefs as truth, even if they are not logical. There are some who fit in and do question what the collective reality believes to be true, but most people will find it easier to just agree and go along with what they are told. Those who find themselves not fitting in are forced into a position of questioning what others do not bother taking the time to consider.

Gay people, or anyone else who is judged as wrong by a religious collective reality, are automatically forced into a position of questioning some of the closed-minded ideas that religious beliefs inject into our culture and politics. This is because we know in our hearts that our attraction to the same sex feels right, and we know how we want to express ourselves, but many of us will grow up facing beliefs that tell us we are wrong for following our inner desires. People's attitudes toward gays are generally becoming more positive, but judgment stemming from religion remains a powerful influence, and unfortunately an influence that generally describes those who are gay as abnormal. As long as condemning aspects of religion continue to influence our culture and our politics, we must be vigilant of the collective reality they are trying to create. There are of course churches that benefit and support gay people, but we must be careful in becoming too complacent when so many churches remain judgmental and even condemning of gays. I'm sure we have all heard of the crazy minister who has become lost in their misconstrued and warped ego perceptions and begins to teach their parishioners to hate and even harm gays. These bad actors face little accountability for their actions from the greater religions they are a part of, so we must be the ones to speak about the injustices they preach.

Questioning Reality

"Being gay is natural. Hating gay is a lifestyle choice."
—*John Fugelsang*

For us gays, the most obvious question to the religious collective reality is: why would God disapprove of us and condemn us to hell for having an attraction we are born with? Many of us felt a same sex attraction starting at a young age, and some of us even tried to deny our gay tendencies by hiding them, even from ourselves. In our youth, most of us had to pretend to be heterosexual if we wanted to be accepted and liked by our peers or to continue to feel loved by our families. Many of us were successful in acting straight, but we knew being gay was not something we could change. We could only pretend or act as though we were someone else, which eventually became mentally draining. When we came to the realization that we would be living a lie the rest of our lives if we didn't accept who we were, many of us gained the courage to come out to others. It was by going through these types of experiences firsthand that we know for a fact that we did not choose to be gay. It was not a choice we made one day just so we could purposefully go against our family's expectations and the God they believe in. Yet, this is exactly what many religious leaders and their followers believe we are doing.

There are many things that religious doctrines proclaim to be wrong in the eyes of God, and most of these reflect the opinions of the straight and male dominated culture that existed throughout a religion's history. Of course, many of the historical cultural wrongs listed in Christian doctrine are ignored today, but being anything other than heterosexual still remains a major sin in our religious culture. Why is this? Why would so many other "sins" listed in the bible fall by the wayside, but being gay is still a huge sin? The reason is that many churches have already created a collective reality that is unaccepting toward gays and because this is what they are accustomed to, they do not feel the need to change their beliefs. It's simply easier for people to judge gays instead of trying to understand them.

Further, church leaders may see gays as a threat to their religious collective reality because gays are much more likely to confront and question a belief that does not accept them or that judges them harshly, putting religious leaders and their followers in the uncomfortable position of having to provide logical answers to what appears to be hypocritical to gays. Judging homosexuality as sinful is simply what many religious followers have been taught to do, and it may also make some of them feel more powerful or righteous when they can look down on another person in judgement. So, it's not that the God of the Christian bible deems homosexuality as the "greater sin," it's just that many religious leaders fear having to change perspectives that could lead their parishioners to question their own reality. Further, some religious leaders don't want to admit that they had it wrong all along about homosexuality, because that could potentially open the floodgates of questions concerning other interpretations of their doctrine, and maybe even a call for an apology for all the abuse they have caused gays.

I have seen how some churches are beginning to interpret religious doctrine in a way that is more accepting of gays, but many religious groups remain adamantly against doing so. In the meantime, there is a battle between belief and logic in the United States, and despite the fact that we are supposed to have a separation of church and state, some religious beliefs are still able to overpower logic. Something the gay men and women of the United States fought hard for was gay marriage and it was not given to us by popular vote in most states. Instead, it was a supreme court ruling that chose to follow logic over religiously held beliefs toward gays and make marriage equality the law for all. This of course has put the collective reality of religious zealots into disarray because they see marriage equality as an attack on their beliefs, even though it has no real effect on their personal lives. So, instead of try-

Questioning Reality

ing to be more open minded and accepting of logic, they seek revenge by whittling away other gay rights and protections. They do not need demeaning laws and limits to gay rights, it does not truly affect their personal lives. They want laws to reflect their own religious views so they can feel they have control over their reality by controlling how others are treated in society.

> *"It takes no compromise to give people their rights…it takes no, money to respect the individual. It takes no political deal to give people freedom. It takes no survey to remove repression."*
> —Harvey Milk

It is painful to see that some people have no compassion for what gay men and women have had to go through, especially in the past. Historically, gay men and women had to live secretive lives and meet in discrete ways to express their desires and love for one another. They had to live in a state of perpetual fear because being outed could lead to torment and condemnation. They could be jailed, placed in a psych ward, have their homes vandalized, be evicted, be physically attacked, be fired from their jobs and even be disowned from their families. It's heartbreaking to think about the abuse gay men and women have been put through, and it's even more heartbreaking that it still continues for some today. Despite the role hate still plays in our modern times, many western perceptions are changing, and thankfully, outward hate toward gays is no longer the social norm—although it still happens.

Spiritual Pride

Along with the change in social norms toward gays, our modern technology has enabled us to find power in our voices because we now have the ability to quickly communicate with one another across the world. This allows us to speak of the wrongs we experience and shine a bright light on hateful acts—acts that are sometimes intended to be hidden from the public. With the greater ability to research in depth, we are able to track down the behind-the-scenes sponsors of hateful rhetoric and refuse to support the brands and people who promote it. With connections and money come power, and two things gays can come together on are funding good causes and closing our wallets to the sponsors who hide behind hate.

We have come a long way toward being accepted as part of the collective reality rather than labeled as something wrong with it, but the plight to be seen as respected people continues. Being accepted allows us to live more freely in the modern cosmopolitan world and because of this, we do not have to spend so much of our mental time trying to hide who we are or trying to figure out how to survive when being exposed. The ability to live openly is a long and continuing battle, and the gays that came before us fought hard for us to experience the luxury of a free mind—something they could only dream of having. Some of us may not even think about the idea of a free mind because we have always had the experience of having it, but it is a precious gift that allows us to better understand and fully enjoy our lives. For example, when we are now able to live in suburbs and go to restaurants on a date without being stared at, we are provided a peace of mind that was unheard of for gay couples in the past. This peace of mind takes us from existing in a perpetual state of survival mode that took up much of our mental energy, to being afforded the opportunity to explore more of who we truly are. A free mind affords us the mental time to read, study and explore in a deeper context the meaning of our lives. This includes developing a spirituality that resonates with who we are and our experiences, something that would have been very difficult to do historically.

Questioning Reality

As more and more people begin seeking the true origin of hate toward anyone, the more they will understand that the origins of hate are man made, not God made.

As gays begin experiencing more of a free mind, we can spend more of our mental resources seeking a greater existential understanding of who we are and why there came to be so much judgment against us. For those of us who choose to begin a spiritual journey of self-discovery, we discover a reality in which gays are a beloved part of Spiritual Source and we see that homosexuality is a unique spiritual experience in itself. Discovering this spiritual truth will lead some of us to want to know why the current day collective reality came to believe that being gay is wrong and inferior to being straight. To do so, we can look into the copious amount of historical information that provides a different narrative than what religious teachings have provided.

Belief has long been used as a source for money, power and control. Now it is time for people to wake up and bring love and compassion back to belief!

Non-religious historical accounts show that for centuries people have been led into a system of thinking that was created by a lineage of heterosexual men who had an agenda for power and control. This patriarchy wanted to suppress gays from having any power or any pride in themselves, so they used God as an excuse to condemn us. Yet, the true source behind condemnation is not from a God at all; it stems directly from the ego desires of the ruling patriarchy. Many of these controlling men considered women to be weak and inferior and any male who was effeminate was also deemed as such. A powerful man being in touch with his femininity could be a threat to a chauvinistic culture.

Spiritual Pride

A woman who did not produce offspring did not serve her purpose of making a new king or more children to create their future armies. A strong and intelligent woman posed a threat to the male dominated power structures and she could be killed simply by calling her a witch. Yet, these beliefs are not based in truth, they are created by the minds of humans, and they are still in a way being perpetuated in today's collective reality.

Collective realities are constantly in flux; they grow in logic and sometimes they step away from it. Until the current collective reality becomes more aware of their own irrational beliefs stemming from past ideologies, people will need to protect themselves against the ills that can happen as a result of them. As for gays, this means that we will continue to need laws to protect us against those who direct their hateful beliefs toward us, and we will need these laws until people become more comfortable questioning the rationality of their beliefs. We cannot force a judgmental collective belief to change, but we can express the need for protection while also helping to inspire people to question the beliefs that are hurtful to others.

The greatest human achievement would be to create a collective reality that is both compassionate and understanding of all of humanity—something the gay community has worked very hard to do.

BORN THIS WAY: A SPIRITUAL EXPLANATION

"Homosexuals are not made, they are born."
—Abhijit Naskar

I believe a majority of gays are born with the innate drive to be gay, but some of us definitely choose a gay relationship later in life. Either way, whether we are born to be gay or choose to be gay, it should not matter. Being gay is not a sin and being gay is not less than! It is a beautiful life experience and it's in perfect alignment with Spiritual Source. Being gay is part of our Souls' unique journey. It is not less than spiritually, so it should not be considered less than by other humans. A gay experience is a perfectly divine experience!

Spiritual Pride

There is no one way to explain physical attraction or what leads to it, but there is a strong societal influence for boys to act like straight boys and girls to act like straight girls. Without the strong influence that our culture places on gender rules and expectations, I would not be surprised if a larger number of people who currently define themselves as straight were in fact bisexual or pansexual. But, for now, a strong persuasion to fit in with the collective ideas of what is expected for boys and girls is the current reality for most. Thus, acting and being in denial is what some of us must do to fit in and appease the expectations of those around us. Some of us gays were so good at acting when we were younger that the people around us thought for sure it had to be a choice we made one day to be gay. Yet, when those who are close to us get past their denial, it's likely they will look back at some of our mannerisms or the actions we took in our youth and see the telltale signs of us being gay.

In order to explain why some of us are born gay, we fist need to delve into the spiritual concepts that can help provide us with a better understanding. If the spiritual concepts I present do not make sense to you at first, it is ok, I am presenting a new way of looking at life and these concepts will unfold in more detail throughout this book. Opening our minds and seeing things through a spiritual perspective is a process, so do not worry if it takes more time for these ideas to resonate with you. Also, if you already have your own spiritual views about why we are born gay and they resonate strongly as your truth, then live by your own truth! We are human, and it is beautiful to have our own unique perceptions, so this could just be another interesting perspective for you to ponder.

When it comes to spirituality versus religion, spirituality is something that grows with our scientific understanding while religion tries to contradict it. Because of this, the greater our scientific understanding becomes, the greater our spiritual comprehension can become as well, while the gulf between science and religion will continue to grow. Metaphysics is a discipline that applies what we understand scientifi-

Born This Way: A Spiritual Explanation

cally to spiritual concepts and this is why I believe that metaphysics is the best discipline for explaining who and what we truly are. Thus, the spiritual explanations for being gay that I present in this book will be based on my studies in metaphysics and the research I have conducted as a result of what I have learned.

Metaphysics agrees with the scientific view that we are energy, which allows us to get a clearer perspective on how we can exist in both non-physical and physical lifetimes. Metaphysics teaches that we humans are energy. Our thoughts are energy and our bodies are energy that we feed with energy from food. The earth and the universe we exist in are also made up of various frequencies of energy, and this energy is all connected and held together by Spiritual Source. Spiritual Source is not like the energy we associate with heat and electricity; it is all encompassing energy that has a conscious awareness to it. It wills to create the universe we live in and our physical bodies. It wishes to have an experience. It forms the bond that connects us all to one another energetically, and to all other things–physical and non-physical.

We all have an aspect of Spiritual Source within us called our Spirit. It is the true eternal part of ourselves. Our non-physical Spirit exists in a state of loving unity with all other Spirits and together they make up what I refer to as Spiritual Source—what religion would refer to as God and heaven. Our non-physical Spirit exists in a state of all knowing, because it is aware of its connection to everything, and in this state of awareness, knowledge and experience are shared collectively. With connection to everything and all knowing, it is difficult to have a unique experience, and this is why our Spirit comes into a physical life. Our Spirit chooses to forget everything that we truly are and have a human experience under the influence of a separate ego mind—a mind that leads some of us to believe that our human life is all that exists and sometimes all that matters.

Our Spirit does not come fully into our physical human existence; part of it remains non-physical. What connects our Spirit in the physical body to the rest of our Spirit in the non-physical is our Soul. Soul is the connection we have to our greater Spirit or non-physical self. This means that part of our Spirit is in our physical bodies bringing us life, while the rest of our Spirit remains in the non-physical. It may sound strange that our Spirit can exist in more than one place at one time, but we must remember, what appears to be physical and separate with our eyes and through the touch of our bodies is nothing more than condensed energy that appears to us as a form. In reality, nothing is truly solid—including ourselves. Our human eye is simply an organ that detects light frequency and creates what our brain interprets as real objects that we assign a name, and what we physically feel is nothing more than condensed energy that has come tightly together. Thus, to understand ourselves spiritually, it is helpful to be open to the idea that we exist as energy. Everything is energy that humans assign a meaning to based on what we have observed.

(Spirit residing within Spiritual Source)

$\updownarrow$

Soul

$\updownarrow$

(Spirit in human individual)

It's all one, our Spirit can exist in both non-physical and physical realms simultaneously. What connects our non-physical Spirit to our human Spirit is the Soul.

Born This Way: A Spiritual Explanation

It's OK not to have an understanding of being Spirit in our lifetimes. Our Spirit chose to forget and be born into a human experience with a fresh slate to create a unique experience. Human life is a magnificent unfolding, it allows our Spirit to express itself in beautiful and unique ways. We can be completely non-spiritual and live a loving and fabulous life. It does not matter to Spiritual Source if we believe in anything or not.

However, on the downside, if we don't recognize that we are Spirit here to have a free-will experience, we might feel as if we are not being who we "should be" or feel too confused about our human experience, leading us to become fearful, angry or even depressed.

We all have free will to believe as we choose, but those of us who do recognize that we are a Spirit having the experience of being human will better understand the purpose of our lives. With this understanding, we can find comfort in knowing that we are never truly separate or alone when we know that we are an aspect of our Spirit having a physical lifetime—still connected to Spiritual Source through our Soul. We also can allow ourselves to shed the ego limitations we put on our human experience and begin living our lives more fully, without fear and doubt. Instead of living in a state of unknowing, we can feel empowered to express ourselves authentically because we realize that following our hearts' desire is what our Spirit came here to do. We came here to experience this life as we are, not to hide or change who we are!

Regardless of what experiences we have in this life or how much we understand about it, when our own awareness reunites with Spiritual Source, the experience is loving, and we once again feel connected to all that is. Reunification with our spiritual home has been described to me as a big hug or a loving embrace. We no longer function through the limited perception of an ego mind, and we no longer feel separated or confused. We return to the all-knowing truth of Spiritual Source, which only consists of positive and loving energy. A person's sexual preference will no longer exist when their awareness returns to the

Spiritual Pride

non-physical Spirit because we no longer have a gender. In Spirit, we feel a loving sense toward everything, and since every other Spirit in the non-physical also exists in a realm of loving energy, our awareness is reunified with all that is—Spiritual Source.

During our non-physical lifetimes, our Spirits all exist together in a state of unity. This can be hard for our minds to comprehend because as humans, we see everything as being individual and separate. To help grasp this concept, I find it helps to imagine a vast ocean that has many currents. You can think of our Source as the ocean and our Spirits as the currents or streams—together they make up Spiritual Source. In a large ocean there are many paths that the currents and streams of water can take, but ultimately, they all make up one body of water. Now try to imagine if you can that we each have a unique Spirit, but they exist in togetherness to make up what is Spiritual Source. Each Spirit has unique energetic traits that lead them to take on their own direction and have their own paths, such as coming into a human body and having the experience of an individual journey. Remember, we humans are not separate from our non-physical Spirit, we are connected to it through our Soul. Thus, our non-physical Spirit experiences the feeling of separateness and the experience of being physical through us, but in the non-physical it remains in a loving togetherness with all other Spirits.

I know this can be hard to comprehend. This is how the concept was explained to me by my spiritual guide and even I still have a hard time visualizing what this looks like with my human mind. Ultimately, it does not matter, we are not here to figure out our Spiritual home; in fact we cannot entirely understand it with our human minds. We only need to focus on allowing our Spirit to enjoy the experience of being human. You do this by following what you feel in your heart—your desires. So, do not worry if you can't make sense of Spiritual Source. All you need to know is that you are a loved Spirit, and you will return to a loving and beautiful experience beyond your human imagination.

Born This Way: A Spiritual Explanation

No matter who you are in this life, no matter what you did in this life, and no matter what you know or don't know, your awareness returns to a loving and eternal existence.

Now that we have an idea of what our Spirit, Soul and Source are, and how they are all energetically connected, I can better explain the spiritual path of being gay. Ultimately, being gay stems from our Sprit wanting to have a gay lifetime or gay experience. This does not mean our greater Spirit is attracted to one sex over another because Spirit does not have a gender or think with a human mind. Instead, being gay, for many, is an innate path the Spirit chooses to take when it enters the mother's womb. Our Soul connection allows for our greater Spirit to sense the energy of the physical environment surrounding the forming fetus, and this is when a path for our human lifetime is created.

From the very beginning, when our Soul connection was created in our mother's womb, there were energetic factors in our environment that may have led our Soul to create an innate desire to be gay. None of these reasons have anything to do with a genetic malfunction or something else mentally or physically wrong with the fetus. Instead, a Soul may choose a life path of same sex attraction because of the fearful thoughts that the mother or father have while the baby is forming.

For instance, if a mother or father has a fear of gayness, the energy of their thoughts can actually influence the Soul to choose an energetic path or attraction that will lead the child to be gay. This could stem from the parents fearing gay people, their own gay tendencies or having a gay child. Let me explain. Spiritual Source and the universe in which it works seek to balance energy and negative feelings toward gays or anyone else. When there is too much negativity or unbalance in an Earthly environment, Spiritual Source can sense this through the Soul. Thus, if human parents think fearful or hateful thoughts (which are unbalanced) while their baby is in the womb, the Soul of the baby detects this energy and may then choose a path that counteracts or challenges that negative energy. In the case of parents who are thinking or feeling negatively toward gays, the Soul may choose to bring forth a life path of being gay as an opportunity to balance the negative energy it is born into.

Thus, being gay is sometimes a result of the Soul choosing to show the way for those who harbor fear or hatred toward gays–showing them that there is a loving goodness in what they are condemning. People are more likely to open their minds and see being gay in a more positive light if one of their children or loved ones ends up being gay. This is one of the ways the Soul attempts to lead others into being more compassionate and accepting, which helps to balance the negativity in an environment. The gay child grows up, positively raising the energy of the negative environment the baby and Soul are born into.

"Every single courageous act of coming out chips away at the curse of homophobia. Most importantly it's destroyed within yourself, and that act creates the potential for its destruction where it exists in friends, family and society."
— Anthony Venn-Brown

Born This Way: A Spiritual Explanation

Many times, but not always, a gay male child will also display a humorous personality, be fun loving, and show effeminate emotions such as being sensitive and empathetic to those around him. While some gay females will challenge irrational patriarchal rules and customs by showing how women can be strong and independent. Both gay men and women are typically advocates for human rights and acceptance, further balancing energy.

The idea of the Soul choosing a path to positively raise the energy around us sounds good from a higher spiritual perspective, but it can be extremely challenging to be born into a hateful or a closed-minded family. And the spiritual journey of bringing a loving and positive awareness into the family does not always end in noticeable success. Yet, our Soul does not experience fear; it experiences everything from a higher perspective, so it does not fear the idea of having a challenging life. Spirit, along with Spiritual Source, do try to assist and support our human perception and experiences if we allow them. They will not interfere with our free will, so this is another good reason to become aware that they exist and learn how to ask them for more of their loving assistance and support.

Our non-physical, spiritual existence does not need balance; it always exists in a loving state of awareness and unity with all that is.

Humanity develops through our learning and understanding, so sometimes we need to be shown over and over that when we become too negative in our thinking, we become unbalanced and further out of alignment with Spiritual Source, which is always in a loving and balanced state. In the case of judging the experience of being gay—the more fear and hate that exists toward gays, the more gays will be born as a result. Here lies the irony for the hateful people who preach being

Spiritual Pride

gay is wrong—the stronger their hateful beliefs are, the stronger the urge will be for a Soul coming into this lifetime to be the very thing they hate.

There are many paths the Soul chooses to take because all Soul experiences and journeys are unique. As for choosing to be gay, it can be a continuing path the Soul takes over many lifetimes to teach love and understanding, or it could be to assist with balancing energy. Still other times, it's just an experience the Soul wishes to have. I am sure there are many other reasons that I still do not know, but it doesn't matter, no one needs to know all the reasons why energetic paths are created in our lifetimes. All we need to know is, being gay throughout one's lifetime is a journey the Soul chooses to take, and since the Soul is part of the divine, then being gay is divine and an experience that is loved by Spiritual Source.

"Find out who you are and be that person. That's what your Soul was put on this Earth to be. Find that truth, live that truth, and everything else will come." —Ellen DeGeneres

OUR GAY JOURNEY

Gay men and women share a commonality in being gay, but we are all on varying spiritual paths that lead us to having different experiences and ways of expressing ourselves. We can really get a glimpse of this large array of expressions when we gather together for large events such as pride parades. Here we can see styles ranging from preppy to punk, femme to masculine, bears to twinks and lipstick to butch—there are so many other forms of expression we could add to this list! Beyond self-expression, we may also find shy personalities along with really big personalities—hello, drag queens! So yes, we are all quite different in how we express ourselves, but we all share similar journeys of struggling with acceptance and being able to express who we are without judgement or harm.

It's important to note that our personalities or forms of expression are not the same as our ego thinking, but they do blend together to create our unique human experience. Whereas ego is the mind of thinking, personality is our behaviors and mannerisms, so having a propensity to be butch or femme is part of one's personality. How we choose to judge or stereotype butch or femme comes from our ego perceptions. While our ego minds can develop and change with our life experiences, our personality stays with us throughout much of our lifetime. My personality is talkative, inquisitive, fun-loving and open minded. These are traits I have had throughout my entire lifetime, while my ego perceptions have changed many times as I have mentally evolved. For example, I went from having an ego that was very judgmental of others when I was younger to being more loving and accepting toward others as I have grown as a person and in my spiritual awareness. I was not born to be judgmental, I learned how to be judgmental, so it was something I was able to become aware of and then work on changing.

Our personality is the unlimited filter through which the human experience happens. Our ego mind is what adds the limitations.

Our Spirit does not have its own separate personality; it can only experience having a personality when it is involved in a human lifetime. Spirit has a personality through us. When a Soul connection is created in a human body, the Soul chooses inclinations or personality traits that will allow for our Spirit to have a unique human experience. Our personalities set the stage of our human existence. Our ego way of thinking is not part of the experience our Soul chooses, it is only a learned way of "human" thinking that we develop throughout our lifetime. Our Spirit wants to experience this human life as much as possible through the filter of a human personality, but our ego minds learn how to judge ourselves and the world around us. If we happen to develop an insecure or fearful ego mindset in our lifetimes, it is likely we will limit who we allow ourselves to be or what we allow ourselves to do. Unknowingly, we allow our ego thinking to become a detriment to our own human experience. If we are unable to become aware of our own negative ego thinking, it's likely we will continue to repress our own innate personality, as well as the experiences we allow our Spirit to have.

Our journeys of being gay can vary greatly because we are instilled with various personality traits that combine with our ego ways of thinking—thinking that reflects our culture and our personal experiences. We will come together at parades, bars and events to celebrate being gay, but we will each go home to different lifestyle circumstances and ways of thinking—sometimes very different. We may also view the gay events we attend together with very different perspectives that can sometimes lead us to not getting along. Despite how our personalities and lives differ, most all of us will have touched others in a way that has helped them to open their minds and to see beyond their learned prejudices. We have a tendency to be compassionate and patient with those close to us who do not understand why we are gay because we realize they are not taught to understand it. While growing up gay, we are not taught much of anything positive about being gay, either. Our own experiences help us see the positivity in being gay. Because of this, it can be hard when we are younger to explain the reason for being gay to others; we don't really understand the reasons ourselves. Yet, in trying to explain to others, we may help bring clarity to our own existence, while also making those close to us question their own judgmental beliefs.

The energetic traits of the Soul can influence a general life path or what some call a purpose, but the human ego can be very strong. Our ego thinking may lead us to make decisions based on our experiences and education that will dictate our everyday choices despite our innate desires. For example, a person's learned fear of being gay can be so strong that their ego mind will try to override their innate sexual desire for the same sex. This is because a person's ego fears being judged or not accepted, so they try to ignore their sexual desire and keep themselves from acting upon it. However, this will likely lead them to feeling very conflicted and when sexual desires become very strong, it's likely they will act upon them in secret, leading to guilt and shame.

Choosing to give up on our authentic desires is not looked down upon by our Spirit or our Soul, which instilled the desire. Our greater Spirit does not judge us and is completely unaffected by our ego decisions, but we will likely suffer a detriment to our own human experience. People who forgo following their Soul's innate desire to instead fit in with ego cultural expectations are not being authentic to themselves. They create an internal conflict between inner desire and expectation. This can lead to a difficult life. How we each choose to live our lives is ultimately up to us as individuals. There is no spiritual mission we are here to accomplish, we are just here to have the experience of being human. Just being human can be a feat in itself, so we do not need to add further expectations to the experience. The universe does seek balance, so there will be energetic events that occur on a personal level or a collective level to assist with balancing energy, but this is a natural process our Soul practices. It does not come with the expectation that we have to do something.

Our natural environment exists in a state of balance because nature is not under the influence of an ego mind, but humans can be ruled by their ego thoughts, which have a tendency to become unbalanced and negative. If ego were not balanced, then humanity would have the propensity to become very negative and destructive. A world ruled by negative ego would be a world that exists in despair and destruction, and humans would become so locked down in closed mindedness that fear would be the norm—freedom of expression, speech and lifestyles would be squashed. There would be a limit on creativity, art and music, and people would not be able to choose who they love. How do we know that a world ruled by an unbalanced ego would be like this? Because in various places on this Earth today, it is like this! We can look at some cultures on this Earth today and see how the people are very unbalanced; free will is suppressed, rights are taken away and the people live in sadness and despair. The people of these cultures may fear for their lives daily and because of their tyrannical, egotistical leaders, they become targets for war and destruction—it's indeed very sad to witness.

Souls can come into the existence of a loving society while others come into a closed-minded and negative culture or family. This is not a spiritual punishment or reward, this is only the result of humans creating environments through their own free will. Because of this, a Soul that chooses to be gay in a very closed-minded culture will likely find a very difficult path. It's quite likely the person who is born with a gay tendency in this type of environment will have to hide their inner feelings or they too may succumb to the negative ways of their culture. The frustration of not being able to live according to their inner desires may lead them to act out in anger or even violence toward someone who has the courage to be their authentic gay self.

As I have said before, we are born into families that are the way they are because of ego; there is no God controlling how certain cultures exist. If we are born into an unloving and negative culture, it's because humans created that environment through their own free will. The result can be that certain cultures will have ruling egos who enforce the continuance of a downtrodden and closed-minded culture. If this is what some cultures choose to be like on a collective level, neither Spirit nor the rest of the world can force them to change. However, Souls will come into areas of the world where free will has been taken away to bring forth loving energies in an attempt to balance it.

This is for a higher purpose. It is not a punishment to those who are born to be free-spirited and loving. Hopefully in time and with enough numbers, people who are inspired on a Soul level to live freely will come together to voice the need for change. Other people should not forcefully try to change an unbalanced and negative culture, but if these cultures try to exert their negative will onto other free will societies, then unfortunately we may have to stand up to stop their uninvited negative influence.

So now that we are really seeing the difference between spiritual truths and manmade judgement injected into beliefs, why would any of us want to hold back from enjoying our lives or acknowledging our spiritual journey? We should be doing exactly what it is that brings us joy and feel divine in doing it. If it feels good, it is right. Yes, there may be pushback and judgement that comes from other people, but when we love ourselves and we live by our own truths, negativity coming from others will affect us much less. Also, we more easily rise above people's ignorance and resume our path of seeing the joy and beauty in living when we know we are loved and supported by Spiritual Source. There will always be those who look down upon our lifestyles, but in reality, they are looking up to us from the mud and yuck of fear and hate in which they wallow. We need to stand proud and on higher ground, knowing we are right in being ourselves. The energy of our love is in alignment with a balanced universe, and hate is what is unbalanced and thus out of alignment.

What brings us closer to Spiritual Source and a healthy state of well-being is finding joy in being exactly who it is we wish to be.

Hate can lead a person to lash out and hurt others, but it hurts the people who inflict it the most. People who focus on hate are likely to dwell on negative thoughts that make their own minds sick and tortured. Spiritually speaking, hateful people like to preach that gays are not worthy of a loving higher connection, but the reality is that their hate is what isn't worthy. Homophobic people can try all they want to make the God they believe in hate us, but a hateful God will only exist in their own hateful minds. We must stand up to the injustices that hate can bring, but in our own minds we can stand strong in knowing that when we love ourselves and others, we are in alignment with Spiritual Source and the universe in which it operates.

No matter what any of us gays have experienced in this lifetime, it is so very important for us to not become jaded and resentful or fall into being hateful ourselves. Life can be difficult, but we can find courage in knowing we are right in being who we desire to be. This knowing can help us pick ourselves up and choose to love ourselves and others, rather than turn to hate and revenge. We do not need to lower ourselves to the level of being hateful ourselves just because we have felt the wrath coming from other people. Hate creates its own form of prison—a prison of the mind. When we free ourselves from focusing on hate, we free our minds from its prison.

Some of us may get to a point in life where we are unable to decipher if the feelings we have are legitimately our own or if we have been taught to feel them. This is because from the time we are young we are programmed with so many beliefs, each telling us how we should be. To discover our authentic selves, we have to discover what beliefs have been imposed upon us and separate them from our own true thoughts and feelings. Anyone who finds that they are not sure how they truly feel because they have been exposed to so much outside influence can know this: if something they want to do makes them feel good, then it is authentic; if something they are doing does not bring them joy, then they need to question why they are doing it. It's very likely they can trace the reason back to some ego ideology telling them how they are supposed to act and feel.

Spiritual Pride

What is most important for anyone who lives a gay lifestyle to know is that our life journey is beloved. Spiritual Source doesn't see us as different; it sees our experience as beautiful. We will be told we are wrong by other people and we will be told by them how we should be thinking and feeling, but these are not ideas coming from a judgmental God. They are human ideas coming from human minds. When gays, just like anyone else, express themselves fully in a joyful and creative way, the energy around them becomes loving and positive. This is what Spiritual Source senses as being in alignment and balanced. The positive energy of this experience is what Spiritual Source sees as beautiful.

"We need to judge less and understand more."
— Mitta Xinindlu

Think of how beautiful this life journey could be for all of us if people would just stop judging others as less than and stop trying to push their superior views onto others. As gays, we need to stand proud in the face of homophobic judgement because those of us who choose to follow our hearts and be happy are the ones living truthfully.

It's not just heterosexuals judging gays. We gays can be quite judgmental of one another, too. The habit of judging is contagious, and some of us are quite guilty of paying judgement forward. Perhaps because some of us are so judged in our own lives we may develop a tendency to project that judgment onto others who have a similar journey as ourselves.

Or, when someone who is gay does not fully accept themselves as gay, they may judge others who are happily expressing themselves. An example of this is when a gay man describes themselves as "straight acting." If they are using the term to describe themselves as more of a man then they are implying that straight men are real men and gay men are not. Thus, to be a real man, they must act overly masculine or "straight." But, the reality is that a true man is in balance with both their feminine and masculine sides. Some of us do use the term straight acting to describe things we like to do that are considered heterosexual activities, or in reference to more conservative dress, but there are plenty of gays who are in touch with their feminine side that enjoy these things as well. We can all have our own preferences, but we do not need to be mean or aloof with those who want to express themselves in their own unique way. Going forward, let's all try our best to be compassionate and accepting of ourselves and of another person's gay journey, OK?

"Judging a person does not define who they are. It defines who you are." — Wayne Dyer

PERSONAL POWER

When we think of what it looks like to have personal power, we may at first think of someone who is very beautiful or has a lot of money. Perhaps a pop music icon comes to mind or a billionaire. In some sense, they do have an outward appearance of being powerful since they can afford to do more of what they want and have a larger platform to be seen and heard, but this is not the same as personal power. Personal power comes from within us, it is feeling worthy and valuable; it is having pride in ourselves and a sense of belonging. Ironically, some of the people who have an outward sense of power can still feel insecure and unworthy on the inside. They seem to have it all—the looks, the money and a glamorous lifestyle—but they still may not feel powerful in their own skin.

Personal power is something we naturally develop when we are young; it is something that we are led to feel by those around us.

Spiritual Pride

The development of personal power begins with feeling appreciated, loved and accepted by our families and our peers. It comes from being encouraged to act and feel just as we want to act and feel. It is being told that we are right in being whatever it is we want to be, and it comes from being honored for being our authentic selves. Unfortunately, this is not the reality for many people growing up, and it's especially not the reality for most of us who come out as gay. Many of us gays did not grow up with a sense of feeling appreciated or accepted for being true to ourselves, which was a detriment to our developing a sense of personal power as a gay person. Instead, we may have found that love and respect were given to us on the condition of being straight, which those around us considered normal in society and right by God. So, for us to feel loved and accepted, we may have had to sacrifice our authenticity. We may have acted in a way that matched the expectation of being straight. Or maybe we were strong willed and faced getting battered and bruised for being open with who we truly were. Whichever path we chose, many of us were emotionally scarred and disempowered when we were told by our peers, our families and the faiths that we grew up with that we are wrong for being who we were born to be. Instead of being led to believe that we were perfect for being who we were or that we are loved just as we are, many of us were made to believe we were unworthy and abnormal—we were led to believe that if we chose to be ourselves, we would suffer a hard life.

Being led to believe we are wrong for being who we are shakes our young foundations and diminishes our ability to feel powerful in our own skin. Since many of us were not supported in our choices or encouraged to be our authentic selves, we were led into a tailspin of self-doubt and feelings of unworthiness, especially during the process of coming out as gay. While many of our heterosexual peers were supported and encouraged, even if they did not make the best decisions, we may have found that we did not get the same treatment. It's more likely a young heterosexual person will have their failures seen by others as ordinary struggles that come with life, whereas our failures and misfortunes may have been seen as expected because we "chose to be gay." Also, when our heterosexual peers felt down or cast out, they were more likely to find a faith that supported and encouraged them to get through the hard times. A supporting faith for gays was not readily available to most of us, so we did not experience the benefit of spiritual answers that traditionally give people confidence in feeling perfectly created as they are.

Because we were taught that God does not love gay people, we had to find or develop our own beliefs in ourselves. Because of this we may have mistaken a belief in ourselves with a need to prove ourselves. As a result, we were more likely to look for perfection in success, physical appearance, style and demeanor.

As adults, this will lead some us to believe that if we can create material success in our lives, then we can also love ourselves and be loved by others. Unfortunately, no matter how much outward success we create for ourselves, the scars of being told we are not worthy can persist. Perhaps we shove these feelings deep inside and refuse to look at them, but when we have our dark and lonely moments, the pain caused by these scars may come to the surface, haunting us with a nagging sense of not feeling worthy or good enough. Yes, we are quite capable of creating outward success for ourselves, but we may still feel uncomfortable and insecure in our own skin. We can hide behind all our outward labels of success all we want, but if we don't truly love ourselves or believe in ourselves as worthy, we are failing ourselves on the inside.

In our lifetimes, many of us do find our personal power and feel valid for being who we are, but some of us may never find it. It doesn't matter when we discover our personal power, it just matters that we do. But how do we find love for ourselves if we have been indoctrinated to think we are less than, or that we must be good looking or successful to be worthy and acknowledged? The answer begins with developing a belief in ourselves that transcends the limitations of our human ego thinking. When we understand that we are part of something divine and eternal—loved for expressing what we truly feel in our hearts—this knowledge permeates every aspect of our lives. It empowers us with a belief in ourselves that goes beyond our ego thinking and any of the insecurities created by it. By knowing that we are accepted and loved by Spiritual Source, the force behind all that is, we are empowered to live our lives authentically and with courage—the courage to be exactly who and what we want to be. If the most powerful force in the universe loves us unconditionally, then there is no reason for us not to love ourselves as well!

"If you don't love yourself, how in the hell you gonna love somebody else?" —RuPaul

When we begin seeking a spiritual belief that empowers us, some of us may at first look to religions or churches that don't condemn us. They do exist, but we will also find that they don't offer a scripture that includes or directly supports us either. Many religions didn't recognize gayness when they were created so they don't mention any outright condemnation of it. But since they didn't acknowledge homosexuality, it's also likely they don't have any doctrine to provide support for being gay either. If you were to ask some of the leaders of more accepting religions whether the lack of condemnation in their scripture means that they are supportive of gays, you may find that they do not directly support homosexuality, but often they do not condemn it either. Take the Dalai Lama, for example, who is the leader of Tibetan Buddhism. It has been noted that when he was asked about homosexuality he has been vague in his answers—he does not condemn it, but he does not offer direct support either. However, he is a human rights advocate and he has openly said that gays should be protected against abuse, and for that I am thankful. It appears to me as though many of today's accepting spiritual leaders will offer their support based on current societal attitudes toward homosexuality, thus as people become more accepting, so do they.

Much of religious scripture is up for interpretation, after all. Most of it has been translated so many times that it can be difficult to know the true original meaning. Some of us will interpret biblical scripture in a way that makes us feel included while others will look at religious doctrine, along with the churches who espouse it, with disdain. No matter what our opinion of organized religion is, the debate will go on and on within religions about whether gays fit in or not. We can leave them to their tireless debate and move on to seeking a spiritual truth that is both supportive and empowering to us.

"What other people think of me is none of my business."
—RuPaul

An empowering faith that is supportive of gays already exists, and it has always existed beyond the banter of religious leaders and the chatter of their parishioners. The love and support coming to us from Spiritual Source has never waned, it has never faltered, it's just that we were taught that it didn't exist for us. The simple truth is that Spiritual Source loves gays just as it loves all people because we are all part of and eternally connected to it. All people at their core—their Soul level—are a loving aspect of Spiritual Source. We all come from the loving energy that is Spiritual Source; this is why feeling love in our lives feels so good to us. When we feel the emotion of love strongly in our presence it is the greatest reference to what our Spiritual home feels like. Love is the only feeling that exists for Spiritual Source. Fear and hate are emotions held onto by humans only; they are learned through the human experience and they do not exist in spiritual realms. Judgmental qualities are taught to be an aspect of the God some religions have created, but nothing condemning or negative comes from our true Source, no matter how much a person preaches that it does. We need to become wise to these human ideas of a God being against gays and gain personal power by knowing with all our hearts that being gay is not spiritually wrong; instead it is a divine spiritual experience, an experience chosen by our Soul and supported by our Spirit!

The reality is, Spiritual Source does not judge our human actions, nor does it have a human type of mind to do so. We are always connected to Spiritual Source and through the connection of our Soul, it knows how we feel or what we are focused on through the energy of our thoughts and feelings. Our thoughts and feelings have an energetic quality to them, or frequency, which many spiritual teachers will refer to as a vibration. Thus, our positive thoughts and feelings are of a higher vibration while our negative thoughts and feelings are of a lower vibration. The contrasts between good and bad experiences that lead us to think and feel positively or negatively do not exist in heavenly realms, there is only the experience of a loving high vibration.

For humans, if something brings us pleasure, Spiritual Source feels the energy of the experience as being high vibrational or loving. If a condemning human decides that to be gay is wrong, Spiritual Source senses their condemnation as negative or an energy that is of a low vibration. The higher the vibration our thoughts and feelings, the more in alignment they are with the high vibration of Spiritual Source; the lower the vibration of our thoughts and feelings, the more out of energetic alignment we are with the good will of Spiritual Source and the universe it works through. Because hate is out of alignment with the loving higher vibration of Source, a person will stand alone in their hate—it is a human feeling that exists entirely outside of Spiritual Source. Being in alignment with Spiritual Source matters because energetic well-being flows to us from the connection we have with it. Spiritual Source does not choose who this energy goes to because it flows to all of us. We open ourselves to it by moving beyond our ego thinking and becoming more loving and accepting, or we create resistance to this energy by becoming lost in our negative and judgmental ego thoughts.

Gays are loved by Spiritual Source just as we are, so gays should never feel guilty if we are doing something that we find to be pleasurable. Our culture, which is heavily influenced by religion, programs us to believe that sex for pleasure is wrong. The underlying belief behind this is that if it's not for procreation, it is bad. We may not consciously agree with this, but for some of us, the idea that sex is dirty is programmed into our subconscious mind, leading us to feel guilty after having sex or self-pleasuring. Especially when we are young, many of us will harbor shame or feel dirty after experiencing sexual pleasure, so when our sexual hormones calm down, we may want to mentally get away from the act as quickly as possible.

Despite being raised to believe God (and Santa, of course) are always watching each and every action made by all 7.7 billion of us on Earth, the truth is, God does not have eyes. Spiritual Source feels our energy, so if someone feels a sense of guilt because they were taught that what makes them feel good is wrong, then Source feels their energy as negative because guilt is a negative vibration. Gays need to feel powerful in knowing that if consensual sex feels good, then it is spiritually in alignment with all that is good in this universe.

We should always feel good about sex and enjoy self-pleasuring if it is something we like doing. In fact, we should feel completely spiritual and powerful in our own skin while doing it, after doing it and when fantasizing about it! Further, we need to feel empowered in all of our choices that make us feel good because anytime we feel good, we raise our vibration and bring ourselves into a greater alignment with Spiritual Source. When others judge feeling good as wrong, we need to know with all our hearts that their negative judgment is what is out of alignment with Spiritual Source, not us.

Spiritual Pride

We can be the light of our own lives, and when we shine bright, we shine the love of our light upon others.

Truly knowing we are part of Spiritual Source and always connected to it is a great foundation to help us begin stepping into our personal power. What is more powerful than knowing we are a beloved part of that which created the universe and all the life that inhabits it? Once we understand that we are a magnificent part of all that is, we begin to realize we are supported in every positive thing we do. This leads to us to feel powerful in our own skin and feel more loving toward ourselves. Just as important, learning about our energetic connection to Spiritual Source is the basis for understanding that we are co-creators with the universe—we energetically create the trajectory of our lives. This concept is going to be expanded upon in the following chapters because what we think and feel plays a huge role in how we will experience our life!

Since the universe communicates and interacts through energy, when we love ourselves and love others, we align ourselves with Spiritual Source, and in doing so we open ourselves to receiving more love in our lives. The connection that results from having a loving vibration is what allows us to receive the healing, inspiration and creative ideas that always flow to us from Spiritual Source. When we are in this flow, life just seems to be easier for us; doors seem to open more easily for us on our daily paths. When we exist in this state of mind, people will come to us and ask, "why are you so happy?" and "why does everything seem so easy for you?" It does not matter what we do for a living, where we live or what we look like. What matters is that we have recognition of our personal power, our loving connection to Spiritual Source and our divine right to be here having this gay experience. Once we discover this as the basis for our personal power, it can never be taken away from us! It becomes an unshakable foundation for the belief we have in ourselves!

"I think being gay is a blessing, and it's something I am thankful for every single day."
—Anderson Cooper

HEALING

While we seek a greater truth to our existence and develop our spiritual foundation, we may also want to take a look at the emotional baggage that we carry from our past experiences. When we allow our ego minds to dwell on our past dramas and pain, we are keeping these past experiences alive in our minds. Doing so takes us away from enjoying our lives more fully in the present moment, and it creates a resistance or block to being in the flow of energy coming to us from Spiritual Source. Nothing stands in the way of receiving this flow of energy but ourselves—our own negative ego thoughts. So, while we grow in our spiritual understanding, we can also work on expanding our ability to receive well-being from Spiritual Source by being in the present moment and healing our resistant ego thoughts.

Many times, we allow the feelings of our past to continue to influence us simply because we don't understand how to address them and overcome them. Not to mention the fact that addressing them head on can be an uncomfortable experience. With spiritual growth and understanding, we start to feel more confident and powerful in our own skin, giving us the courage to take a look at our painful memories and resolve them for good. We release the painful feelings that we associate with our memories by having compassion for ourselves, working through forgiveness, and assigning a more positive meaning to a past event. This allows us to overcome feeling upset or troubled when a past memory comes into our awareness; instead of feeling upset by the thought, we will continue to feel a sense of well-being that helps keep us in the flow of divine energy.

Taking a look at painful emotions

We may be who we are today partly as a result of our past grievances, but we certainly do not have to hold on to the emotional pain caused by them. Some of us believe that we are stronger by not acknowledging our pain, but ignoring it is not a strength, it is a weakness. If all people made a conscious effort to heal their minds from the inner pain they carry, there wouldn't be so much anger and animosity toward one another in the first place. When anyone tries to hide from their inner pain and act as though they are unaffected, the pain will come out in other ways such as withdrawal, anger, impatience, rudeness and a lack of compassion. It is sad that some of the most hurt people in society become difficult or even painful to be around, and as a result they end up living lonely lives, isolated in their pain.

It may seem as though the painful experiences of our past are inescapable, but the reality is, the way we look back at our past experiences is a choice we make. Past experiences do not have to define how we feel now or how we feel in the future. If we have a tendency to focus on past negative experiences, it likely stems from a learned behavior we picked up from our parents or someone else in our lives who was also prone to do this. Learned behaviors, including how we deal with emotions, are passed on from one human to the next, from generation to generation. It is a learned human behavior because holding onto painful emotions and experiences has nothing to do with our Spirit. Our Spirit does not carry pain and hurt, it's only our human minds that choose to do this. Thus, painful memories do not continue on with our Spirit after physical death because memories are not real things, they are just thoughts that we chose to keep alive in our own ego minds.

It is not just our own experiences that can lead us to carry negative emotions; it comes from all around us as well. From the time many of us are young, we are exposed to the anger, hurt and frustration coming from our families, our peers, our leaders and even our news stories. It is difficult for us to avoid being programmed by the emotions of fear, judgement and pain because the stories promoting these feelings are so prevalent in our lives. But it's so important to become aware of this programming, because when we indulge in the painful stories of those around us, we can feel the emotion of someone else's experience and absorb these emotions into our minds as if they were coming from our own personal experiences.

It is possible to listen to the stories of others and not become emotionally involved or take on their emotions as if they are our own. The key to doing this is to remind ourselves that their personal experiences are not part of our own personal path or truth. We are all on our own journeys in life, so we can be compassionate toward the misfortunes of others while not taking on the negative feelings that are associated with their experience. It just takes an awareness of how people project their feelings outward and the choice not to take the energy of their emotions on as if they are our own. We can listen to them and be compassionate, but we don't have to live their truth; we can choose to live our own story.

All people will have to face painful emotions at some point in their life, but gays tend to experience negative emotions persistently throughout our lifetimes. We can be judged harshly, excluded, disowned and even physically attacked just for being true to ourselves, but much of

Spiritual Pride

this happens while we are young and have not yet found our tribe, or even a safe place to live. Once we become established, most of the negative emotions we incur as a result of being gay won't actually stem from something that happened to us personally. Instead, most of these negative emotions will come from seeing stories about the abuse and judgement of gays in the news. Because we are able to learn about the mistreatment of gays on a global level, what other gay people (who we identify with) experience can feel very personal to us—even though sometimes what happened is so far away from us.

We certainly should show compassion and do something to help those in distress if we can, but if we internalize the feelings stemming from all of the stories we witness as if they are our own, we may become a big bundle of nerves and a walking repository of painful feelings. Depending on the story, it can also make us angry and resentful, leading us to lash out at those who are not as sensitive to the wrongdoings as we are. An attack on one gay can feel like an attack on all of us, but it does not serve us in any way to hold onto or internalize negative emotions stemming from other people's experiences. Instead, we can keep our mental energy focused on positive ways to help ourselves and others to create a better and safer future for us all.

"My pain is not caused because I am gay. My pain was caused by how I was treated because I am gay."
—Eric James Borges

Healing

In an attempt to appear strong and unaffected, we may push negative feelings deep inside our minds to hide them from our awareness, but this does not make them go away. Instead, the emotion of negative memories festers behind our conscious awareness and can spread to other areas of our lives, coming to the surface in our relationships, and through our own personal triggers. Our painful emotions are not always readily reached, but if we continue to ignore our emotions, we may find ourselves one day unable to get in touch with who we truly are or how we truly feel.

On top of that, our unresolved painful emotions can lead us to feeling insecure, depressed, anxious, lonely and jaded—feelings we generally want to avoid. But please know, the emotions that cause these feelings have no power over us if we take the time to recognize them and release them. If we find that we have been experiencing destructive behavior or we've been self-sabotaging, we can find peace in getting to the source behind these actions. If anyone feels they have destructive or self-sabotaging behavior, they should not feel like they are unworthy, not strong enough or that there is something wrong with them. It is common for anyone who is carrying pain to want to create another pain or a distraction in order to avoid the painful feelings they carry within themselves.

David's story

To give an example of how an unresolved painful past can affect one's future, I will talk about a time in my life when I did not know how to address or deal with the pain I was carrying—in fact, I didn't want to acknowledge it. I thought I was strong in ignoring it, but it was affecting my life from behind the scenes of my conscious awareness by making me angry and very anxious.

I was showing signs of being gay in middle school, but no one seemed to notice until I moved from Ohio to Virginia and began attending a new school. I never thought of myself as acting differently, nor did the kids I grew up with, because, well, they grew up with me and they were used to how I acted. But, when I started going to a new school, my gay mannerisms and voice were easily picked up on by the other kids in my classes and the teasing and bullying began immediately.

I was singled out by a large number of classmates who wanted a target to project their anger and frustration on and there wasn't anyone who stood up for me or had my back. I was called "fag" on a daily basis and during some of my classes, my classmates would stare angrily at me and mock me. My belongings were constantly messed with and no one would dare sit with me at lunch. I even had a gross guy pull his penis out in math class and ask me if I wanted it. It happened more than once, and it was very uncomfortable and demeaning.

It was a really tough time for me and an experience I had not encountered before in my life. It was very unfortunate that I was scared to say anything to my parents or school counselors because I was worried they too would think that I was gay or weak. I was ashamed, so I tried my best to not let them know what was going on with me at school. I wasn't ready to admit being gay to myself, and especially not ready for my parents to begin thinking it too. Luckily, I only lived in this new school district for eight months, and then we moved back to Ohio. But, that eight months of being in Virginia felt excruciatingly long when I was going through constant torment and rejection at school. Being judged and demeaned is such a horrible feeling and I hope most of us never have to encounter it, but unfortunately for me, it became part of my childhood story.

I was not bullied as much in high school because I learned to keep a low profile and hide who I was by dating girls, but there was still name calling and I was never chosen for any team or included in much of anything. Despite the lessening of name calling and degradation, the mental damage was already done, and it was not being helped by

Healing

me feeling excluded. I was carrying around internalized shame, feeling as though I was less than, and I worried that if people found out that I was gay I would be humiliated, demeaned and even attacked; in fact, I expected it.

I only experienced a few negative encounters in college as a result of me being gay, but the culmination of my past experiences and the internalizing of my hurt feelings led me to begin having physical side effects. This included high blood pressure, social anxiety that was sometimes debilitating, excessive sweating and a heart that would begin to race uncontrollably when I walked into college classes or anything institutional.

I also needed to drink alcohol just to relax and be myself with my friends. After college, the feelings resulting from being ashamed of who I was and from trying to hide my gay mannerisms carried on, making it difficult for me to find a job because I would become debilitated with anxiety prior to an interview. I expected to be judged and I expected to be dismissed or rejected. The unfortunate thing for my mental health during this time in my life was that I did not see the correlation between the negative experiences I had encountered and the onset of me developing intense anxiety, especially around schools and workplaces. I just figured that there was something wrong with me physiologically—that I was just biologically predisposed to anxiety.

Beyond high school and college, I made some really good friends and I had a ton of fun at the gay bars and clubs. I found lots of people who, like myself, had been repressed and who were now ready to really have fun expressing themselves. I could be quite charming when I was partying, but I could also become the drunken mean guy, acting out and judging others. Sometimes I displayed arrogance to hide my insecurities, and if I was crossed I could become overly angry because I hurt so deeply. The hurt was hidden just below the surface and I would project the wrath of this pain onto others if it was triggered. I was a bit of a mess at times, so it's no surprise I also attracted messy boyfriends or the bad guys. This led to tumultuous relationships, and because I was hurt by my first few boyfriends, I became calloused in relationships.

I have always been on a mission to be happy, but I carried the pain associated with my gay youth way too long—even into my early thirties. My search for happiness was hampered by self-sabotage as I verbally attacked and projected my pain onto those I loved. I erroneously blamed those around me for my pain and I would unfairly make them feel as though they were the cause. Looking back, I didn't know how to equate my actions as a direct result of my attempt to hide from my inner pain, and if I did, I didn't know then how to deal with it. Eventually, I could not continue to overlook the nagging sadness and pain coming from inside me. I was being someone I did not want to be and acting at times like the people in society I felt embarrassed for. This is when I decided enough was enough and I chose to begin doing self-help work, get counseling and begin a meditation practice. By making a choice to do these things, my life changed. Boy did it change! I will share what I have learned from my experiences, and if it helps anyone else on their path to healing, it's my honor!

Working through our emotions

I realize some of the pain of our past transgressions can be intense and if anyone needs help addressing these emotions, please look into getting a professional counselor. A counselor can guide and comfort a person through the process, but it is we alone who have to do the mental healing. No one can do this for us.

The first thing we need to do when working through our past traumas or negative emotions is to take some time for ourselves. This does not mean taking a vacation, going to the spa or going shopping. Yes, these things can help us to relax and can make us feel good, but what I am referring to here is taking some time to be alone with ourselves and get in touch with how we feel. Checking in on our feelings is a great way to determine if we are carrying around any unresolved emotions that are leading us to act out in other aspects of our lives. When we scan our emotions, we may come across something that we didn't think bothered us, only to find out that indeed it did. We may have moved on and ignored how the event made us feel, but we can see now how the negative emotions persisted behind the scenes of our awareness.

When you choose to begin working through your emotions, find a quiet and comfortable place to sit alone with yourself, or have a trusted friend/family member with you. Try and do this when you feel level headed and relaxed; it's not healthy to delve into emotions after a night out drinking, a stressful event, or when we are tired; these things lead to being mentally unbalanced. Ironically, these are the times when most of us do acknowledge our inner emotions because we are less able to consciously suppress them, but it really is not the best time to address them.

When you are ready to get started checking in with your emotions, begin by taking long, deep breaths—deep breathing helps to relax the body and calm the mind. This is the process of getting ourselves grounded; being grounded helps make us feel secure and feel that everything is OK. As you breathe, focus your attention on relaxing your body, especially on any part of yourself that feels tense or uptight. Continue this process of deep breathing and relaxing each and every part of yourself until you find yourself peacefully relaxed. Know that right now you are in a safe space and you are taking this time to give yourself loving thoughts and healing energy.

Now focus on your emotions and move your attention to any thoughts that come into your awareness. You may feel good feelings and thoughts coming into your mind, and of course that is wonderful, but if you feel stressful or painful thoughts coming into your mind, now is the time to give them your full attention. If the thought immediately causes you distress or anxiety, it is beneficial to breathe

Spiritual Pride

deeply because this helps to counter anxiety and continues to keep you grounded.

Once we discover any negative emotions we are holding onto, there are several ways to go about releasing them, we just need to find what works best for ourselves. The methods to help with this are: having compassion for ourselves, reassigning a more positive meaning or emotion to a past event and working through forgiveness.

Having compassion

When a painful memory comes into your mind, do not try to relive the painful details of the event. Instead, focus on having compassion for yourself in the moment. If the event was caused by your own actions, it's important to remember that we all make mistakes and choices in life that we regret, and it's possible that through our own pain and suffering we acted out on someone else. We are having an imperfect human experience and we grow through our mistakes as well as our successes. Be compassionate by reminding yourself that life can be difficult and challenging, especially when we are younger, but even as adults. Most of us were not handed information or guidance on how to be gay or how to navigate the experiences that result from being gay. We had to learn many things on our own and we carry our pain and frustrations silently through these experiences. It's normal to look back and find the reasoning behind your actions, but it serves no beneficial purpose to beat yourself up about it. It's very likely that you grew from the experience and you now see the experience in a way that you could not see it before. Be thankful for the ability to grow from it, but do not be hard on yourself for what you could not see at that time.

"Our sorrows and wounds are healed only when we touch them with compassion." —Jack Kornfield

Assigning a new feeling to the past event

In doing this, we are literally attaching a new emotional meaning or feeling to a past event—an event that does not even exist anymore except in our own minds. Assigning new meaning does not change what happened, but it changes how we feel when we reflect back on the memory. It also changes how the memory can affect other aspects of our lives by eliminating the anxiety that stems from a past situation. I wish I could tell you how to delete past events from your memory entirely, but what has happened has happened and memories do not typically just go away. So, when looking back at a painful memory we want to heal from, we acknowledge that we are choosing for it to no longer have any negative affect on us by assigning a feeling of love and compassion for ourselves instead. We choose in this moment to love ourselves and give ourselves loving support for what we have experienced. When thinking about a past memory, we can affirm something positive such as "I am powerful and loved," "my body is safe and loved," or "I have grown into a wiser person." What we are doing here is assigning a positive feeling to our past experiences, so that when these memories pop up in our awareness in the future, we will feel the positive emotions of strength and self-love rather than feelings of anxiety and pain.

We absolutely have the power to release the negative feelings attached to any memories and reassign them with positive feelings instead. Our minds only assign emotional meaning to past events that we once gave to them; now we are assigning them with something new, something positive. The memory may arise in the future, but we will feel less pain or no pain at all coming from the past situation. Life is a journey; it has its ups and downs. We make mistakes, we learn, and we grow. Negative experiences are only kept alive in our minds if we so choose, but in reality, they don't even exist. This life is our drawing board, so we should go forth and experience the feelings that we want to feel in this moment.

Forgiveness

While having compassion for oneself is one of the best ways to heal from our own past actions, forgiveness is a way to move beyond the negative emotions that we feel stemming from the actions of another. Forgiving others, especially those we placed our trust in, or for things that happened to us as children, can be difficult because we can't always make sense as to why people do what they do or did what they did. Forgiveness does not require us to see the perpetrator's side of the story, but it does help us to understand that what they did likely stems from ignorance or from their own anger, frustration and pain. Likely, either they were programmed with negative behaviors or something bad happened in their own lives that led them to acting out or doing something to harm another; it's the people who are hurt or misguided who act out in a negative way toward others. We do not have to put ourselves in their shoes to understand their actions; instead we can forgive them for not having experienced a more positive way of existing. Their actions and their way of being result from their own issues and it truly has nothing to do with us. We can forgive them for not knowing better and focus on releasing the negative energy of the situation, so that it does not continue moving forward with us.

    I realize forgiveness can be difficult, especially when some of the experiences we have had at the hands of another are very offensive and painful. The horrible things people do to others is never OK. Yet, we can choose to give loving compassion to ourselves for going through a bad experience and focus on how it made us stronger as a person. We can also choose to forgive a person who is living a life of pain and misery that would lead them to hurt someone else. This does not require us to reach out to them or speak to them; we forgive them in our minds, that is all that is necessary. They are on their own journey and if they seek forgiveness from us they will ask. When looking back at past situations that make us feel upset and vulnerable, it's good to remind yourself that you are physically safe in the current moment. What hap-

Healing

pened then cannot hurt you now, only the memory of it has any power over you—a memory you are going to take control of.

How we each choose to hold onto memories differs, but if we choose to replay the pain of it over in our minds we are keeping the negative event alive. Some of us will use our past pain as a badge to describe the things we had to go through in life and how we are stronger because of it, but those things only make us stronger if they make us more compassionate toward ourselves and others. If our experiences have made us bitter, resentful, jaded or condescending, then this is not strength, this is hurt—hurt that we may now pay forward to someone else. This is misguided strength that serves no one, and if we find ourselves carrying pain as a badge on our sleeve, we really need to make peace with ourselves—with our memories.

When we work through past painful memories, there are many techniques we can use to assist in the process. I will explain some of the tactics I have used, but you may find your own methods for helping you to release emotions—you may even develop your own technique!

Writing out your feelings is a great way to discover what you are holding onto, and through writing you bring your hidden emotions to light. After you have written out your feelings, you may find it helpful to take what you wrote and burn it because this is a powerful representation of release. By destroying the words that describe your pain, you make a powerful assertion that you will no longer hold onto this pain; it no longer has any effect on you. During my time of healing, I used to do what is called a full moon release, meaning that each time there was a full moon, it served as a reminder for me to write out what I no longer wanted to hold onto. After writing these thoughts onto a piece of paper, I would go outside and read out loud what I wanted to release and what no longer served me, and then I would burn the paper.

Another technique for releasing negative feelings attached to a past memory is to use affirmations with breathing. For example, affirm to

Spiritual Pride

yourself, "the energy of this situation no longer serves me, I choose to release it." Take long deep breaths as you do this. With each intake of breath, imagine you are breathing in strength and healing. With each exhale, visualize yourself releasing the negative emotions from your mind and body. If you doubt the power in doing this, you should know that your mental intention is the most powerful thing that exists! Behind every creation is an intention—everything starts with a thought. Not to mention, deep breathing will relax your body and mind, leading you to feel a sense of well-being.

The last technique I will discuss is to enlist the power of your Spirit during the process of mentally healing. If you could see Spirit with your human eyes it would appear to you as white light, so visualize a loving white light coming into your presence, one that protectively surrounds you. Then imagine this white light coming into your mind and surrounding the memory to help heal the pain of it. You can use the breathing technique I just discussed in conjunction with this. Imagine breathing in the healing white light of Spirit and when exhaling, visualize Spirit taking away the negativity. Sound far-fetched? Well Spirit does indeed help, it does have the power to help balance our energy, physically and mentally! If you intend for it to happen and believe that it will, Spirit is here to comply.

There is much power behind the thoughts we focus on because we are not separate from our Spirit. It just appears as though we are separate while having a physical experience. In terms of energy, we are always connected, and if we believe the great power of our Spirit can help heal our minds, then it absolutely will—and so it is! Remember, this is a free will human experience, so Spirit does not help unless we ask.

We are powerful in our own right and while we are in physical bodies, everything begins with a thought or intention.

Healing

A note on negative programming

Just as knowledge is passed from one generation to the next, pain, anger, fear and resentment are also passed on. This is called mental programming, and if we happen to be raised in a negative or toxic environment, it's likely we too are picking up the habits of negative thinking. Because negativity can be the "normal" behavior in our lives, we may not understand the ramifications it can have on our attitudes and thus our personal energy. If we don't realize the patterning of this, we may also emulate this way of thinking and acting ourselves. We too could become contributors of passing on this way of thinking to others, including the next generations. It is like a negative domino effect, or negatively paying it forward.

When you recognize thoughts or feelings that don't resonate with how you want to think and feel, then you are catching on to how you may have been programmed to think and act a certain way. For example, if we did not like how our parents thought about certain things when we were growing up, but we now find ourselves thinking similar thoughts, then we are acting on programming. We need to focus on how we want to think and feel. When the thoughts come into our minds that remind us of the way we do not want to think, we need to stop the thought and reprogram it by focusing on our own authentic feelings. There is a part of our mind known as the subconscious that plays a powerful role in how we automatically think and feel, which brings me to the next chapter about our holistic self. In learning to see the whole of what we are, we can focus on how all the parts of ourselves work together and why it's important to keep all parts in alignment with one another.

"Our brains are like computers; it's our responsibility to program them well, daily, and remove the viruses."

—*Sam Owen*

THE HOLISTIC VIEW OF OURSELVES

Having a holistic view of ourselves means recognizing that we are the sum total of our mind, body and Spirit. To live a holistic lifestyle means actively paying attention to the thoughts we entertain, the health of our bodies and the strengthening of our connection to Spirit. It also means thinking about how all of these aspects of ourselves work together to form the quality of our human experience. Following a holistic path leads us to becoming grounded and centered, or in other words, feeling a sense of well-being, health, inner peace and the ability to focus on what matters.

It is not important to have an advanced knowledge of anatomy or neurology to have a holistic understanding. The focus is not on the details of our inner workings; rather it is to strengthen our spiritual connection, make healthy lifestyle choices, and keep our minds healthy by working through our issues and living in the moment. Doing these things prevent negative health issues because when we function in a state of well-being, we help to keep our mind and body functioning properly. Of course, things do go awry with our bodies on occasion, so when this happens, we can leave the details of diagnosing specific physical issues with our doctors and holistic practitioners.

Yes, when things malfunction with the mind and body it helps to go see a specialist, but those of us who want to feel a sense of mental well-being in our daily lives and work toward the prevention of health issues can get started on a holistic journey. Living holistically is a lifestyle choice. To help get you started, I will discuss the mind, body and Spirit and how they all work in conjunction with one another to create well-being in our lives.

"Just because you're not sick doesn't mean you're healthy. Good health is not just the absence of pain or disease but positively feeling good in the whole of our being, and therefore includes lifestyle, mental attitude, and ways of relating to all living beings and nature." —Peter Shepherd

Mind

When trying to describe the mind, most of us will depict it as being the thoughts that come from our brain. This of course is largely true, but we also have a mind that partially exists in other parts of the body, and a spiritual mind that exists in a state of peaceful awareness beyond our ego thinking.

Our **conscious mind** is associated with brain activity and it is what we use to analyze, problem solve, plan, visualize and communicate verbally. In addition to our conscious thinking, there is the **subconscious mind,** which dictates many of our autonomic bodily functions, or in other words, bodily processes that function beyond our conscious awareness. The subconscious doesn't just have influence over our physical bodies, it also influences many of our automatic mental responses to life events. It is guided by the hypothalamus in the brain, but it has activity that spans throughout our body. For instance, the subconscious mind holds onto memories that are stored as energy in the cells of our body. These cellular memories can have a huge influence over the quality of our bodies' functioning.

Our subconscious mind remains active while we sleep, hence our dreams, and it also communicates energetically to our surroundings. Have you ever felt someone watching you? Has the hair on your arms stood up when you walked into a place that doesn't feel right? This is the body acting like an antenna that is subconsciously receiving outside influences and then bringing this information to your conscious awareness. The subconscious mind is also the receiver of intuition because it has the ability to translate energy coming from Spiritual Source into conscious thoughts. Our Spirit is constantly communicating to us, but we "feel" it beyond our conscious awareness.

Beyond our conscious and subconscious minds, we can tap into our **spiritual mind,** which is a peaceful awareness that exists beyond any thought at all. It is similar to the awareness in which our Spirit exists.

Spiritual Pride

This peaceful awareness is something that many meditators experience when they move their awareness beyond their conscious ego thoughts. The many benefits of experiencing this calm and serene state of non-thought is why many meditators will stick with their meditation practice for the rest of their lives!

To help you understand your various mental states, we can think of our conscious mind as being associated with our brain, our subconscious mind as being associated with our body, and having moments of peaceful awareness as tapping into the peace and calm of our Spirit. *Our subconscious mind is ultimately controlled by the hypothalamus in the brain, but we notice the quality of its functioning through our physical well-being and our automatic mental responses.*

It is easy for us to recognize our conscious thoughts because they are the thoughts we focus on in the current moment. Your conscious mind is reading this and determining what it is I am trying to convey. It may be easy for some of us to focus on reading this, but for others, they may have a difficult time controlling the direction of their conscious thoughts and will find their minds drifting off to something else.

While some of us can control the direction of our conscious thoughts, others will struggle with this. Those who struggle to control their thoughts may feel at times as if their thoughts are driving them crazy. If "racing thoughts" describes the state of your thinking, you are not alone. We are programmed daily with a lot of information, and when our minds become overloaded, it can feel as if we are unable to control all the information presented to us. This is why taking mental breaks is so good for our sense of well-being.

Behind the scenes of our conscious thinking is our subconscious mind. Our subconscious mind works differently than our conscious mind, but how it functions is dependent upon what types of thoughts we consciously focus on day in and out. For instance, if we tend to be positive in our thinking, then we will program our subconscious mind

The Holistic View of Ourselves

to be in a positive state of well-being as well. When our subconscious minds are positively programmed, we feel relaxed and at peace, which has a beneficial and healthy effect on our physical body. On the other hand, if we focus on negative thoughts such as fear and hate, then we are programming our subconscious mind to exist in a negative state. A subconscious mind that has been programmed to be negative will be disturbed and it will not provide us a sense of physical well-being. Instead, this kind of programming will have an ill effect on our autonomic nervous system that regulates bodily processes such as respiration, heart rate, blood pressure and digestion. Thus, a negatively programmed subconscious can lead to rapid/short breathes, high blood pressure and indigestion.

Not only does our subconscious influence our autonomic nervous system and our physical response to events, it also influences the quality of our conscious thinking. Many of our mental responses to life events are automatic, meaning they come from our subconscious mind rather than our conscious thinking. The subconscious is the source of our knee jerk reactions. I'm sure most of us have had an inappropriate thought about something pop into our minds, but we stopped ourselves from consciously saying it. This is an example of an automatic subconscious thought coming into our awareness that we consciously monitor. The subconscious mind can even take over doing certain things while we space out or daydream. Ever find yourself driving on the highway and after a while, you realize that you were not paying attention to your driving? That's because you were on autopilot, or in other words, your subconscious took over while your conscious mind zoned out.

It's not just our own thoughts that can program the quality of our subconscious minds. What we watch on television and the opinions of the people we choose to listen to can also be programmed into our subconscious minds. This is important to take note of because outside influences programmed into our subconscious mind can lead us to think and feel in ways that are not authentic to who we truly are. They can lead us to feel at odds with ourselves. This is especially important to consider when listening to media commentators because they have a tendency to project strong statements that evoke our emotions. If their opinions are very angry or judgmental, then we invite their negativity to become an influence on how we think and feel. We may not consciously agree with what they are saying, but if we choose to keep listening to them, then their ideas are literally becoming a part of our own subconscious thinking.

If we choose to listen to people who rile us up with fear and judgement, then we may find that our own automatic responses to life take on a fearful or judgmental quality—perhaps we begin overreacting to little things. We may look back and consciously think, wow, I can't believe I responded to someone or something like that, but if we have been allowing ourselves to be negatively programmed, then our subconscious mind is likely the culprit.

We may also get frustrated when we go to do something that we normally should find fun, but we cannot truly enjoy ourselves because of our negatively programmed subconscious mind. What should be a good time is met by feeling uptight, on edge or anxious because we have indulged in fearful thinking that has literally programmed us to feel out of sorts. It could be a Saturday night and we have the intention of going out to socialize and have fun, but now we feel anxious and unsettled because during Monday through Friday we focused on our negative thinking or listened to negative programming.

A tell-tale sign that we are subconsciously carrying around a lot of programmed negativity is how we automatically respond to life events. If we respond immediately with anger or fear to something we don't agree with, or we snap at someone who accidentally steps on our toes, it's likely our subconscious has been programmed to exist in a negative state. Because our subconscious storehouse of thoughts and feelings is programmed with negativity, our automatic responses in life are also now negative.

The Holistic View of Ourselves

We can of course see what others and we have programmed into our subconscious mind when we drink too much alcohol. When we drink too much, we lose our conscious ability to stop our subconscious responses and as a result, our inner subconscious thoughts can come out unfiltered for those around us to hear. But, what comes out of our mouths is not necessarily our truth. Since our subconscious can be programmed by outside influences, what we say may not reflect how we actually feel or think when we are sober. There can certainly be a discrepancy between how we consciously think and what is programmed into our subconscious mind, leading us to say and do things that are not reflective of who we are or how we currently think and feel.

To be more in alignment with our own truths, we need to be cognizant of what we allow ourselves to focus on. We must determine if what we choose to indulge in is really in alignment with who we are or how we want to feel. We may discover that we once held a type of opinion, but now we don't; perhaps there is an entertainer we once gelled with only to find that we don't really get them anymore. In these cases, we may want to stop giving them our attention, or better yet, stop indulging in the opinions of others altogether. Instead, we can spend more time focusing on how we want to feel, and we can choose to spend more time with the people who inspire us and who we wish to emulate.

When we are not sure whether our thoughts are genuinely our own or whether they come from someone else, we need to check in with how we feel. We can do this by taking moments out of our day to ask ourselves, "do I feel good about how I am thinking and feeling when I look at the world around me?" If we find that we automatically respond to life events and other people in habitual ways that don't make us feel good, then we need to stop the thought and ask ourselves, "how do I really want to feel about this, or how do I really want to see the people around me?" Much of how we think is automatic and programmed, but we are master controllers and we have the power to change the quality of our thoughts at will.

Body

We have a tendency to believe that the health of our body is dependent upon our eating habits alone. Because of this, most of us will focus primarily on our diet and less on how we think, believing that as long as we eat well, we will be healthy. Diet is of course very important, but the reality is, our body is also greatly influenced by the quality of our thinking. Over time, the quality of our conscious thoughts will program the quality of our subconscious mind and in turn, the quality of the subconscious mind has an influence over our autonomic bodily processes. If the subconscious is programmed negatively, with fearful thoughts for example, then we are unknowingly causing stress on our body. On the other hand, if the subconscious is programmed to exist in a positive state, then we will feel a sense of well-being because our bodily processes are not stressed by the subconscious mind.

Because our subconscious mind influences much of our automatic thinking and autonomic bodily functions, it is important to understand how it is programmed by our conscious thoughts. If we do not consciously monitor what programming we are exposing ourselves to, or we don't work on healing our emotional pain, we can inadvertently negatively influence our physical bodies. For example, when we allow ourselves to dwell on our own fearful ideas or obsess over the fearful stories coming from the news, this negativity is programmed into our subconscious mind. As a result, we may experience physical anxiety because the subconscious mind of the body is in a stressed state. And because the anxiety is caused by our subconscious mind and not our conscious mind, we are not always able to predict it or control it—which can be scary for us.

The good news is that we can change the quality of our subconscious mind over time by consciously focusing on positivity, surrounding ourselves with positive people and using positive affirmations when negative thoughts come into our awareness. This allows us to positively rewire our brains and the memories held within the cells of

The Holistic View of Ourselves

our bodies. *Because affirmations are so beneficial to programming the way we want to think and feel, I have devoted an upcoming chapter just to affirmations and how to use them.*

As gay people, it is important for us to be aware of the consequences of holding onto the feelings that come from being judged. When we focus too much of our attention on the negative things that other people say about us, our subconscious minds may be internalizing their negativity; we can become a walking repository of some other person's negative words and actions. I do not mean for us to turn a blind eye to people who are negative to us; I mean to not become affected by their words by giving them too much of our mental energy.

When we give too much of our mental attention to their negative verbal attacks, we subconsciously put ourselves into a defensive state of being that can be a drain on our own energy. Instead of using our energy for the beneficial functioning of the body, the subconscious mind thinks we are being attacked and it will work to keep the body in a defensive state. This is what is referred to as the flight or fight response and it can be triggered to stay active by our subconscious mind.

Just by consciously listening to words of attack, we can lead the subconscious to believe we are in real physical danger. The subconscious mind does not know the difference between an actual attack or thoughts of being attacked. The result is, if we spend a lot of time worrying about being attacked, we can trigger the subconscious mind to put us in a defensive physical state of being, leading us to be on edge, be a bundle of nerves, to develop anxiety and perhaps even panic attacks. It takes a lot of energy to stay in a defensive physical state, so the subconscious mind will divert energy that should be used for the proper functioning of our autonomic bodily processes. For example, when our subconscious is programmed with thoughts of fear, our digestion can become upset and our heart may begin to overwork, leading to rapid heart rate and even high blood pressure. Overall, we lose our sense of physical well-being and instead feel nervous, tired and tense.

Spiritual Pride

It is up to each of us to decide how we deal with the stress of our environment, but all of us need to make sure we find balance through self-care and loving thoughts about ourselves and the world around us. The good news is that we can take control of our own well-being by changing the quality of our thinking and what we are allowing to program us. As my spiritual guide tells me, "It all begins with a thought!"

> *"I will not allow anyone to walk through my mind with their dirty feet."*
> *— Mahatma Ghandhi*

Spirit

Spiritual Source exists in a positive and loving state of awareness—always. Humans have the free will to exist in many contrasting states of minds, running the range between love, which is positive, and hate, which is negative. The more we love, the more we feel a sense of what our Spirit feels like; the more we hate, the more we lose ourselves to our ego thinking. Spirit always wants to assist our human experience by bringing us a sense of well-being and intuitive guidance, but we take ourselves out of the alignment to receive it by getting lost in our ego thoughts—ego exists outside of Spirit. To align ourselves more fully with our Spirit, we bring ourselves into the present moment and take our own ego thoughts out of the way. In doing so, we allow the energy coming from Spiritual Source to flow freely to us.

We have free will to choose how we think and feel about our lives, so whether we bring ourselves into alignment with our Spiritual Source or not is a choice we make on our own. A spiritual person who understands their connection to Spirit will allow time in their day to remember their divinity and focus on bringing their awareness into the present moment. They will also focus on perceiving life in a positive way because it has a beneficial effect on their mental and physical health, or the whole of who they are.

As we have discussed, our conscious positive thoughts over time program our subconscious to exist in a positive state, which leads us to automatically respond positively to daily events and brings well-being to the body, allowing the physical body to relax. This relaxing of the body leads to a calmer heart, better digestion, deeper breathings and a relaxed demeanor, which are all beneficial to our physical health. We respond to life's nuances in a relaxed and calm demeanor and we can even see the humor in some of the ridiculous ways people act and think. Further, we overcome negative blocks in our energy and align ourselves with the higher vibration of Spiritual Source, allowing us to receive the beneficial life force energy and intuition it is always providing for us. We do not need to ask for assistance from our Spirit over and over; when we are in positive alignment and are open to receive it, it becomes automatic.

Despite what traditional religions teach us, it does not matter to Spirit whether or not we are aware of its existence in this lifetime. Spirit does not judge what we do as humans as good or bad, nor does it calculate where we go in an afterlife world. What happens as a result of our ego minds in this lifetime happens in a vacuum or illusion; it has no effect on our true spiritual self. To believe we are separate and have a separate experience is like a dream; it's the ultimate illusion we experience while in physical bodies. One may ask, "If it doesn't matter to the Spiritual realms whether we are aware of them or not, then why bother being on a spiritual path or recognizing Spirit at all in this lifetime?"

The answer is, recognizing our true spiritual nature allows us to free our minds from the chains of fear and dread that we may find ourselves in. When we realize we came here to have the experience of living life to the fullest, and not to be put to a test and judged, we can allow ourselves to live more freely and passionately. When we understand how our true spiritual selves are energetic, we can use the energy of our thoughts and feelings to influence the health of our minds and bodies along with what we attract to ourselves. When we know we are always part of our Spirit, then we know that we are never truly alone, and we can put ourselves into alignment to receive guidance and healing from our Spirit at any time.

Spiritual and holistic truths are not readily presented to most of us because these truths are empowering. Some religions were in part created out of the need for a few to control many, and as result, the doctrine needed to be disempowering to the masses. It is important for anyone on a spiritual path to cut the idea of judgement and hierarchy out of belief, but this can be tricky once we have been indoctrinated into this limited thinking. But, as a general rule, take judgement, the need to worship, the need for approval and the need to be on a mission or ascend to a higher existence out of any teachings and you are already headed on a more truthful spiritual path.

It does not matter whether we learn spiritual or holistic information and techniques from others, in books, in classes or we discover how to connect to our Spirit and get it straight from Source. What does matter is that we go forward, exploring and developing our own personal beliefs by finding what resonates with us and what we are comfortable with. Our unique take on beliefs represents each of our unique and special connections (Souls) because Spirit will connect with us in a way that we are each comfortable with. When we find a belief that is supportive and loving, it is the loving vibration that bridges the veil and connects us to home.

For the beginning spiritual and holistic seeker, it may feel out of this world that many Spiritual people who have awakened beyond the illusions of ego can in fact communicate with Spiritual realms. Yet, for the experienced spiritual seeker, this is actually a very normal and natural occurrence. Spirit knows what we are comfortable with or what we can handle, and it will not communicate to those who have shut down this connection due to being indoctrinated into ego thinking.

Most of us are heavily programmed with fear of the unknown, which serves as a block to receiving insight from Spiritual Source. This programming did not happen by chance; it's an old way of keeping us in the dark in order to better control us. As a result, many of us fear what we do not understand, and our fear keeps us in a place of not learning, making it easier for us to be controlled by other people. The good news is that we can awaken to this programming and transcend the grip it has upon our thinking. In doing so we are less influenced by those with hidden agendas and we can see that fearing the unknown is a learned behavior and not a true reality.

Spirit is always around us because we are part of it. We cannot make Spirit go away but we can shut our minds off from recognizing it. Many of us do close down any recognition of our spiritual connection because we have been raised to fear "unseen forces" existing around us. This is no surprise since many horror movies feed on our fears by perpetuating the belief that if we try to connect to our spiritual home, we open ourselves to evil spirits who will then haunt us! It's all just misguided programming that leads us to believe that if we shut our minds off from thinking about what we cannot see, somehow, we are protecting ourselves from some angry ghost or demon. This programming is so unfortunate because evil is a human creation. Yes, it exists, but not in spiritual realms; it exists only as a result of human thinking. Humans can be very cruel, but this is not a result of some unseen force; this is the result of a human ego gone wrong. The non-physical world of Spirit is always loving, and always trying to bring to us what is beneficial and in our greatest good. Our Spirit forces nothing upon us; we either open our awareness to our spiritual connection and receive the love, abundance, wisdom and healing that it offers, or we choose to ignore it.

••••

Having the holistic view that we are our mind, body and Spirit will lead us to a better understanding of who we are and how we are connected to Spiritual Source. With this understanding, we further see the importance of being present, passionate, thankful, appreciative, generous and courageous enough to do the things we desire to do. We all are capable of being on a holistic journey, but we are all unique, so our ideas and methods vary somewhat. So, while on this journey, follow your heart and your intuition; it will lead you to your truth and to your happiness.

BEING IN THE PRESENT MOMENT

"The secret of health for both mind and body is not to mourn for the past, worry about the future, or anticipate troubles, but to live in the present moment wisely and earnestly". —Buddha

We may choose to focus much of our attention on our past memories or possible future outcomes, but when we do, we take our focus away from living our lives in the present moment. The present moment is the only place where we can allow ourselves to enjoy the richness of life and be truly immersed in our experience and surroundings. In reality, the thoughts we have about our future or our past don't even exist. They only seem real because we focus our minds on them. We may feel as though our thoughts about the future or past have an influence on defining who we are, but the only real thing that defines our experience is what is happening to us right now—what we are doing in the present moment. When we focus too much of our mental energy on holding onto the memory of a past event or worrying about what tomorrow will bring, we become lost in our ego thoughts or what I refer to as "living in our heads." When we allow ourselves to live in our heads, we focus our attention on a nonexistent reality that keeps us from truly enjoying our lives right now!

Focusing on the now moment is beneficial to our mental well-being because it allows us to move our awareness beyond the misfortunes of our past and the tension caused by worrying about our future. A relaxed mind leads to a relaxed body, and the only place the mind can find true relaxation is in the present moment. Yes, when we think of fun memories and a dreamy future we can find relaxation as well, but how often do we keep our thoughts about our past or our future strictly positive? It's likely not often, a thousand good things may happen, but we tend to focus on the worst-case scenario or something bad that has happened to us. When we stop to think about it, we may be surprised to discover how little we actually focus our attention on being in the present moment. It could be that we only focus on the present when something in front of us requires our immediate attention or when we are learning something new. But, once we learn a task and it eventually becomes a habitual process, we may begin to complete the task on autopilot–allowing us to go back to living in our heads.

I realize it isn't always easy to focus solely on being in the present moment, even while we are actively trying to. Our conscious minds tend to want to go back to focusing our attention on what needs to be done for our future; while our subconscious minds like to remind us of our past actions. We also look around us and see the environments we find ourselves in that serve as a reminder of our life choices or circumstances that are sometimes out of our control. So yes, it can be difficult at times to just be mentally in the present moment, but it is never impossible.

Being in the Present Moment

Like anything else, focusing on the present moment takes practice, and with practice it does become easier. It requires us to first recognize that we are living in our heads, and then make a conscious decision to focus on what is right in front of us or where we are in this moment. In doing so, we can experience the richness and beauty of life with a fresh outlook that is not clouded by our past experiences or future worries. Being present with ourselves can eventually become habitual, especially when our subconscious minds become programmed to focus on being present.

Of course, many of us have careers that require us to focus on our agendas and our appointments, but in the midst of our work, it is important to take breaks that allow for us to become present with ourselves. When taking a break, replace gossiping or complaining about work with taking a walk, sitting in silence or appreciating something around you that is inspiring. This could entail taking time to notice the weather or nature that is around you. Taking a moment to sense the weather or nature will always bring you into the present because they exist in the eternal present moment. Once you get used to making time for yourself to have mindful moments, you will find yourself wanting to do it more often. Throughout your daily routine, you will be more inspired to take a moment to recognize the little details of beautiful things in your life, even while you are at work. You will want to "stop and smell the roses."

"Unease, anxiety, tension, stress, worry—all forms of fear—are caused by too much future, and not enough presence. Guilt, regret, resentment, grievances, sadness, bitterness, and all forms of non-forgiveness are caused by too much past, and not enough presence."
—*Eckhart Tolle*

Spiritual Pride

If you are a person always on the mental go, analyzing what has happened and focusing on what needs to be done next, then now is the time for you to take a moment for yourself. Find a beautiful space in your home to relax in—perhaps a room that you made to look beautiful, but you have not been taking any time to enjoy. Go to this space and just be present with your senses. Notice the details of what you have created or decorated. Pay attention to the patterns, the textiles or the art in the room. At one time these things caught your eye in the moment and brought you joy, leading you to buy them. Think about how the things around you make you feel right now. By doing so, you just brought your attention into the present moment.

Does everything around you look OK? Have you been neglecting your plants and the need to dust? Yes, realizing you have been neglecting your surroundings can be the less desirable part of bringing your awareness into the present moment. You may be able to overlook this for now, but if you are a neat freak and a plant lover like myself, you may need to take care of some cleaning and watering of the plants first. Once that's done, you can settle back into your comfy space, and check in with your current mood. Does everything feel OK with you? If not, what emotions need your attention? Addressing emotions may take you temporarily out of being in the present moment, but it was taking the time to be present with yourself that allowed for them to come to your attention. If you feel fine or do not want to address your emotions, then now is a great time to just have a mindful moment that brings you to sense the beauty and inspiration around you. This may entail taking a moment to feel a sense of appreciation and gratitude for what you have in your life right now. This is also a good time to just sit in silence or enjoy some soothing music.

Every now and then, we can use the present moment to remind ourselves on a grander scale what this life is all about. We are Spirit wishing to experience life in a physical body. The human actions, thoughts and feelings that happen while we are on this Earth stay on

Being in the Present Moment

this Earth. Their energy does not go with us when our physical body dies. The only thing that goes with us is our awareness, but this awareness returns to an all knowing and loving presence. Knowing this, why on Earth (literally) would we spend our time living in the past or worrying about the future? We are given this amazing opportunity to live in this beautiful present moment and we are given the free will to think and feel as we please!

Some final tips on being present with yourself:

- Take moments to think positively about yourself and see the good in others.
- Let the thoughts of fear and anxiety caused by living in our heads be replaced by feelings of more confidence and security that can be found in being present.
- Forgive yourself and others; it will allow you to move forward in life and be more present in the moment.
- Try to dream about your future rather than worrying so much about it. When you maintain positive desires for your future, Spiritual Source senses those feelings and works through the means of the universe to help us get what we want.
- Know that allowing yourself to be positive in the present moment will help to attract other positive people and events into your life.
- Notice how you begin to automatically feel a sense of well-being when your subconscious mind begins to align with the present.

In this present moment, choose to love yourself, love others, and love your life. You are beautiful, and you matter in this world. We all do!

AFFIRMATIONS

As we have discussed, the subconscious mind acts like a sponge by absorbing the conscious thoughts and feelings we focus our attention on. Because of this, when we entertain a lot of negative self-talk or act judgmentally, this is how we program our subconscious mind to function. If our normal way of thinking has become negative, we do not need to feel stuck in this type of mindset. Instead, we can work on "reprogramming" our mind to improve the quality of our thinking.

To help us initially become more positive in our thinking and also to help us maintain a more positive mindset, we can rely on the use of affirmations. Affirmations are uplifting and encouraging statements that describe how we want to think and feel. They are words and phrases that inspire us, empower us, and lead us to believe in ourselves. We can focus on these positive words and phrases when we find ourselves thinking negatively or when we are trying to create a new belief about ourselves. When we affirm something to ourselves, we are making it our story—we are making what we affirm to be our own truth.

The positive affirmation serves two purposes. First it gives us something to focus our attention on instead of the negative thought, and second, it actually works to reprogram our thinking over time. Our subconscious minds and brains are changeable, so we absolutely have the power to reprogram them. Thoughts are just things we choose to entertain, so if we choose to focus on a positive affirmation, then we are actively rewiring our brains and reprogramming our subconscious minds to match the affirmation.

The result of focusing on positive thoughts and affirmations over time is that we begin to feel more empowered, at peace, courageous, beautiful and loving toward ourselves and others. We also experience a more positive sense of physical well-being: we have a more relaxed nervous system, better digestion, lower blood pressure, a relaxed posture and an overall relaxed demeanor. On top of all this, our automatic responses to life events become more patient, open minded and loving rather than upset and annoyed.

To put affirmations to use, begin by choosing affirmations that describe the types of thoughts and feelings you want to have. Write your chosen affirmations down on a piece of paper and place it anywhere that helps you to remember to focus on them. State your affirmations often to yourself throughout the day (quietly or out loud), especially when you find your mind straying into a place of negative thoughts. It's important to catch yourself when you begin thinking negatively so that you can stop the thought in its tracks—this will help you break the habit of focusing on negative thoughts. Next, move your attention away from the negative thought and focus instead on your chosen affirmation. When doing this, it is helpful to choose an affirmation that counters the negative thought specifically.

Affirmations

We need to keep our affirmations simple and direct so that they are easier for us to remember and focus on. What we focus on becomes our reality.

When coming up with affirmations that make sense to you, pick one that makes you feel good. Even if your chosen affirmation sounds silly and makes you laugh, it is still good—laughing and having fun are joyful and thus positive. If you are not creative in coming up with your own, then search for positive affirmations that match what you want to think and feel. There are plenty of affirmations listed online and some are even dedicated to just gay men and women.

How do you use an affirmation when you are thinking a fearful thought about something you must do? Stop the fearful thinking and then focus your attention on an affirmation that counters the fear, such as "I am courageous," or "I've got this!" We need to remind ourselves that many of our fearful thoughts are learned responses and most of the time they are not based on something in our personal reality. For example, we may fear going somewhere because we heard about someone else's negative experience. Just because their experience was not the best, it does not mean it will be the same experience for us.

Keeping our list of affirmations with us and reading the statements frequently throughout the day is beneficial, especially when we find ourselves feeling down or being negative.

Another time to use an affirmation is when we are feeling unattractive. If this happens, we can stop the thought and replace it with "I am beautiful," even if we don't feel our best today. If we are feeling unloving thoughts toward ourselves, we can focus on affirming to ourselves: 'I am perfect as I am," "I am loved," or "my uniqueness makes me beautiful." This process sounds simple, but we need to remember that our subconscious is listening, and this is our powerhouse mind

Spiritual Pride

doing a lot of mental processing behind the scenes of our conscious awareness.

Sometimes our minds can be relentless in trying to lead us back to dwelling on negative thoughts and reactions, especially in the beginning of the process of trying to change our negative mindset. If we find this to be the case, we need to continue to state the positive affirmation over and over to ourselves until the negative thought dissipates or we move our attention onto something else. Persistence with this process is key, so staying focused on the affirmative statements that describe how we want to think and feel is very helpful.

We should not pick and choose what we want to feel positive about in our lives. It is not effective to work on thinking positively toward ourselves but continue to think negatively toward other people and things. This defeats the purpose of trying to reprogram our overall thinking to be more positive. So, when we find ourselves thinking negative thoughts toward others, we need to stop these thoughts and focus on a positive affirmation that pertains to them. For example: "He/she has their own unique way of expressing themselves;" "I admire that they are being true to themselves;" "I may not understand the path they choose but I respect their free will;" "I choose not to judge;" "I send them good luck in their decisions;" or something more humorous like "bless their hearts."

If we find that we simply cannot bring ourselves to think anything positive about a certain person, then we need to try not to focus too much attention on them. I realize sometimes this is not an option, but we need to try not to dwell on their negative attributes. "If we can't say anything nice, then we should try not to give them our attention!"

One of the most important times of day to pay attention to the quality of our thoughts is in the morning. If we wake up and automatically begin thinking positive thoughts, it's a good sign that we have already programmed ourselves to be generally positive in our thinking. But, if

Affirmations

any of us wake up thinking negative thoughts, especially about something that happened yesterday, then we need to stop the thought in its tracks and begin focusing on our positive affirmations. In doing so, we are helping to positively reprogram our thinking while also setting the stage for our day to be more positive. This doesn't necessarily change the events of the day, although it can help. Instead, it leads us to notice more of what is good around us. When we focus more on the good, then we tend to feel good ourselves, and when we feel good we can "rub off" on others by helping them to feel good, too. The more people feel good around us, the more likely it becomes for us to continue experiencing good feelings in our day. On the other hand, if we wake up dreading our day, we set the expectation to have a bad day. We will look for negative things happening around us that match our dreadful feelings and we will focus our attention on them. We will experience negativity because we expect it!

Unfortunately, some negative experiences are unavoidable, and the more we get out and about, the more likely we are to incur them. Rather than worrying about avoiding negativity, work on dealing with it. We can brush negative things off and move on, or we can dwell on the offensive. How we choose to deal with negativity is up to each of us but when we know who we truly are, and we love who we are, we can more easily move beyond the negativity brought onto us by others.

By realizing that we are all experiencing our own unique journeys, we will see that what happens as a result of other people's choices does not have to become part of our own truth. When someone calls us a derogatory name or does something rude, we need to realize these people are in a miserable state of being. Their way of coping with their own misery is to try and make those around them upset and miserable as well. It makes absolutely no sense for us to get involved and absorb their icky low vibrational energy. We can realize they are trying to project their own misery on to us and we can rise above them by not giving them any of our mental energy. We need to remind ourselves

Spiritual Pride

that we want to stay in a positive state of well-being and that no one has the power to change our mood unless we allow them to!

Love yourself and state affirmations if you need help getting yourself into a loving state, but move quickly past those who don't love or respect you. If establishments you visit allow for negativity, then stop going to them. There are plenty of other places to spend your time and money.

Also, no one can pull our triggers like our friends and family. If they continue to get an intended response by pushing buttons, then they will feel empowered to continue doing it. We need to try to rise above these situations by seeing what they are doing, calling them out on it and telling them "I am not giving you the satisfaction," or "I know what you are doing!"

People who like to pull our triggers may be surprised and even bummed that they can't set us off like they used to. When they realize they can no longer get the intended response from us, they will no longer find satisfaction in doing it. But, if they try to keep it up, they can interfere with our positive mindset and it may be time to "set them straight" or to place them in time out.

Going forward, when you wake up in the morning, program yourself with a positive outlook and expectation. As you go about your day, state positive affirmations to yourself and remember to check in with your thoughts and feelings. If you catch yourself thinking negatively, make sure you replace the thought with an affirmation that counters it. Along with affirmations, think about the good things you can do for yourself and others. Kindness can cause a positive chain reaction—when someone receives kindness, they in turn will want to pay it forward.

"I am beautiful and loved—this is my truth!"

VIBES

I'm sure most of us have heard of the terms "good vibes" or "bad vibes." Good vibes refer to a person, place or thing that makes us feel good—warm and fuzzy—while bad vibes describe a person, place or thing that makes us feel uneasy or uncomfortable. We typically use the word "vibe" to describe what we sense from other people and things, but what most of us don't recognize is that we all carry a vibe about us. The thoughts and feelings that we entertain have an energy to them and what we generally think and feel on a daily basis helps to create our own unique vibe. Depending on the quality of our thoughts and feelings, we can be positive, which is of a higher vibration leading to good vibes, or negative, which is of a lower vibration leading to bad vibes. Some people will have a consistent vibe while other people's vibe may change frequently. It just depends on how steady they are in their thoughts and feelings.

Spiritual Pride

Some people can actually see the energy or vibe around a person and this is referred to as their aura, but most of us just sense or "feel" a person's vibe. For example, my husband's energy usually feels good to be around and therefore I like to be close to him when we are together. But sometimes he carries a lot of stress and burnout from work and I can literally feel him carrying a bad vibe about him. What I am feeling is his stress energy and it can be hard to be close to him, not because he is being difficult, it's just that his vibe is radiating a stressful feeling. I love him, so of course I do not try and avoid him when he carries this vibe; instead we work together to get his vibe back into a positive and relaxed state. This may entail going for a walk, getting him to laugh, doing some type of relaxation technique or giving him some space so he can zone out and relax his mind.

If we want to become more aware of the vibes coming from other people, we just need to practice paying attention to what we are feeling from them rather than focusing solely on what they are saying. When we become better at detecting other people's vibes, we find that sometimes people act in a way that matches the vibe we feel coming from them, while at other times, the vibe we feel does not match their words and actions. Developing our ability to sense someone's vibe can be beneficial because we can better protect ourselves from people who are trying to be something they are not. It also helps us recognize when someone has a bad intention but is trying to hide it from us. When a person's vibe doesn't match what they say or do, it becomes a red flag for us. The energy they carry about themselves does not lie, no matter how much a person puts on a deceitful front.

Sensing other people's energy can also be helpful when we notice that our loved ones are radiating a sad or frustrated vibe, especially when they tell us everything is OK because they don't want to talk about it or acknowledge it. In a case like this, we just need to help comfort them without addressing the issue in the moment. When we sense that someone's energy is sad or depressed, we should not try and

Vibes

force them to tell us why or explain it. It's better to give them the space to talk about it when they are ready, or let it go if they never want to.

It may be easier for us to feel the vibes coming from others than it is to recognize or feel our own vibe. The reason is that we are used to being in our own energy. When we are used to a certain energy, we will notice it less. A person close to us may be able to sense our vibe, but it's likely they will only notice the changes in it. That's because those who spend a lot of time around us will typically have a similar vibe, making our vibe less noticeable to them. Like attracts like when it comes to people's energy and it's one of the reasons why we typically feel a comfortable bond with those around us. If there is someone we bring close to us in our lives who happens to annoy us, then it's very likely there was a superficial attraction to this person—perhaps we were trying to make a professional connection, or we found them physically attractive. Beyond that, our energies are simply not in alignment.

If you are not sure of the quality of your own vibe, there is a simple exercise to help discover it. This entails setting a reminder such as an alarm on your phone to remind you to check in with your thoughts and feelings throughout your day. When the alarm goes off, write down a phrase that describes what you are thinking or feeling in the moment or recently, and write down next to it whether it is/was positive or negative. Make a daily tally of how many positive and negative thoughts and feelings you have noticed throughout your day. If you find that you are thinking mostly positive thoughts, then you can be certain you are carrying good vibes and thus radiating these vibes out to others. If this is the case, you can continue enjoying your positive ways of thinking and feeling.

However, if you discover you are generally negative in your thoughts and feelings, then you can ascertain that you are carrying a negative vibe, and this is what others will feel coming from you. If this is the case, you can refer to your affirmations to help you begin the work of

Spiritual Pride

reprogramming your negative thinking to become more positive. As you keep reprogramming your negative thoughts, you will in time become more positive in your thinking and also begin to carry a positive vibe about yourself.

You may discover that when you decide to change your vibe, your energies are no longer aligned with some of the people you keep around you. If some of the people in our lives do not change along with us, then it's likely the relationship or friendship could eventually fizzle out. This is probably for the best if we are becoming more positive and those around us are choosing to stay in a negative space. Obviously, it can be stressful when we are not in alignment with the vibe of our family because, well, they are family, and many times they are going to continue to be in our lives. In this case, it is important to set boundaries with family to protect our own energy and feelings.

How each of us chooses to create boundaries is up to us, but we need to make sure we create space that keeps us from being pulled into other people's drama and negativity. Ultimately their drama is no one's responsibility but their own. There always seems to be that one friend or family member who is constantly embroiled in drama and looking to broadcast it to everyone else by saying "poor me!" Guess who is continuing to cause the drama in their lives? That's right, themselves!

"Don't allow people into your energy field on a regular basis that you wouldn't want to be like yourself."
— Dawn Gluskin

Vibes

The energy vibe emanating from our body carries with it what you could call a frequency or vibration. This vibration is what other people can feel and also what Spiritual Source feels. Spiritual Source does not look through a set of human eyes; instead it senses us as energy and it feels the vibration we carry. We exist in a higher vibration when we are grounded, at peace, happy and secure, which not only makes us more attractive to other people, but also aligns us to the higher vibration of Spiritual Source. When we feel insecure, angry, unhappy, or tend to be more critical and judgmental, we carry a lower vibration that can make the people around us feel uncomfortable, while also taking us out of alignment with Spiritual Source.

One of the biggest culprits for lowering our vibration is a focus on fearful thoughts. It's important for us to understand this because there are people who wish for gays to live in fear and many times they are successful in leading us to do so. We may be happy in many aspects of our lives, but our energy can become conflicted if we constantly fear being attacked because we are gay. A common fear that many of us share is that the government or some other institution may take away our rights or keep us from having them. Of course, we must take action when necessary to express the need for our rights and use our power to vote and to be heard in protest. But it becomes taxing to our mental and physical health to fear for our security day in and out.

Instead of focusing our daily attention on living in fear, we can focus our attention on rising above ignorance and continue to focus on loving who we are. This helps to keep us in a positive state of mind, and a higher vibration. When we maintain a high vibration, we are more receptive to inspiration that will lead us to creative solutions for working toward equal rights. On the days that we struggle to stay positive, we can use the affirmations: "Love and self-expression are everything right with the universe;" "I am right with the universe;" "Love will win;" and "I focus on positive change and take positive action." These affirmations acknowledge the importance of taking action, but

Spiritual Pride

they help to keep us in a positive state of mind rather than a state of dread, which only serves to weaken us and keep us from receiving inspiration.

We have a beautiful life to live right in front of us and we need to enjoy the life we have created for ourselves. The strength we garnish from flourishing and feeling secure with who we are will propel us to continue to fight for what is right. If we become too focused on the wrongs committed toward gays, we become disheartened and worn out. We lose the energy needed to stand up to injustice. There are those who want us to feel downtrodden about ourselves so that we lose the strength to stand up for ourselves, but we should never give into these feelings. This is the goal of those who find ways to discriminate; it is a form of mental terrorism designed to disturb and weaken those they do not like. We need to acknowledge what they are doing, and resist falling into the negative emotions they wish for us to feel.

We can send help and compassion to those who have become victims of hateful acts, but we must not allow ourselves to live a life of constant fear because of it. Despite any administration's agenda to weaken our rights, the majority of Americans are becoming more loving and supportive of the gay community. We did not open people's minds by attacking those who were taught to discriminate or by feeling defeated by their ignorant actions. We have done this by rising above hate. This has allowed people to see the genuineness of our love for one another and the pride we have in ourselves.

Now that we understand how we carry a vibe or an energy about us, we can expand upon this concept by discussing the law of attraction in the next chapter. The law of attraction is always present and always working because it works through energy attraction; everything is ultimately energy attracting other energy.

THE LAW OF ATTRACTION

The law of attraction is presented to most of us as an easy way of getting the things we want in life that are not obtainable in the moment, but there is so much more to the law of attraction than just this. When we hear about the law of attraction being able to help get us the things we want, some of us get really excited, while others think it sounds completely unrealistic and has no basis in reality. Despite what we believe, many successful people proclaim that their success and wealth are in direct correlation to working with the law of attraction and because of this, it continues to get a lot of attention. Unfortunately, most people who are inspired to put the law of attraction to use will find that it simply does not help to bring them what they want, but this is only because they don't truly understand how it actually works!

    I follow several "Law of Attraction" groups on Facebook and I consistently see people posting questions as to why the law of attraction is

Spiritual Pride

not working for them. They continue to create lists of wants and vision boards telling the universe what it is they want but it just does not seem that it's willing to respond. They ask, "Why does the universe work for some people but not for me?" or "What am I doing wrong?"

What they do not understand is that Spiritual Source and the universe that it works through do not selectively choose from our lists and pictures. Instead, the universe feels who we are and what we want through the vibration of our own thoughts and feelings, not a list on a piece of paper or a board full of pictures. It may appear that vision boards do the work of bringing wants to some people, but if they found success while using them, it was not from the vision board itself. Instead, it was from them actively focusing on the good feelings of having what they want, as if they have it already.

> **The only thing our written lists or a vision board do is remind us to focus on having what we want. The universe feels the good or high vibrational energy when we focus on what if feels like to have what we want, and through the law of attraction, the universe then brings into our physical existence that which matches these feelings.**

If a person chooses to work with a concept such as the law of attraction, it is very helpful if they believe in themselves as deserving and worthy of what they want. If they have doubts about their worthiness to receive, then they create an energetic block to the path of receiving. To attract, we must focus on the good feelings of having what we want, believe we are worthy of receiving and trust in the process. It helps to also be patient, especially if we are trying to use the law of attraction to attract expensive things or large sums of money. It may take longer for the universe to create paths of bringing what we want into our existence, but not always. Sometimes it happens quickly.

The Law of Attraction

Spiritual Source only works through the law of attraction when we focus positive emotions on what we want to have—feeling how good it feels to have it, as if we already have it. It does not respond to negative vibrations in the same way. Focusing on how bad something feels in our lives doesn't bring us something bad. Nor will Spiritual Source bring bad things to someone we focus ill will toward. Wishing ill will toward someone or feeling bad about ourselves only serves as a block to being in alignment with Spiritual Source. Instead of wishing ill will toward someone, try forgiving them instead, and move on in life. Energetically speaking, holding any type of grudge or wanting something bad to happen to someone only serves to keep us in a negative space, which is counterproductive to our own well-being.

There are some who do not wish to work with or believe in the law of attraction, and that is perfectly fine. We do not need to try and attract things to us from the universe, but what we all should know is that the law of attraction is multi-faceted because it works differently for the energies on Earth versus the energies of Spiritual Source. So even if we do not want to work with the law of attraction, it is beneficial to at least understand how it works, especially here on Earth.

Spiritual Source only exists in a state of positive high vibration, but here on Earth, we exist in a state of duality, meaning, here there exists both negative and positive energies. We can only attract positive things from Spiritual Source, but here on Earth we are given free will to create and attract both positive or negative experiences. In fact, we are **always** attracting and repelling other Earthly energies, whether we are aware of it or not. The process of attraction happens behind the scenes of most people's awareness because most of us cannot see the energy of attraction happening, but this energy does indeed exist, and it is always flowing among everything.

When we exist in a positive state of mind, good things in life come more easily to us: it's as if doors open more easily for us in life. This isn't magic, it's our own energetic presence connecting to other energies around us, attracting to us things that are in our best interest that match our good vibes, and repelling those that don't.

Unfortunately, on the other end of the spectrum, if we allow ourselves to be negative, we take ourselves out of the flow of spiritual well-being and we energetically close ourselves off from other positive people and events. We instead attract more negative people and events into our lives.

Before I go any further, it is important to note that I have witnessed, and also experienced myself, negative events happening to gay people who were happy and feeling positive in their own lives. It is unfortunate that some people in society set targets on those who they feel should not be allowed to enjoy their lives, believing instead that they should suffer. Here on Earth, like does attract like energetically, but in the case of a hate crime, a negative person just hates a person they don't like seeing happy. Thus, it is important for gay people to understand that the discrimination that we experience is not a result of the energy we carry, or because of something we did. Instead, we are being attacked or discriminated against simply because someone does not like us enjoying our sexuality or our form of expression.

As long as there is hate, we must be vigilant. But we should not expect negativity to come to us for being gay. Expecting it puts us into a negative state of mind, which actually may attract negative scenarios in our lives. Yes, hate can happen, but it's not healthy to focus on it or feel as if it will always happen just because we are gay.

There is certainly an energy of attraction that works for all people, and in some cases what people experience as a negative feeling coming from others is a response to their own energy. But, there are those who will target us just because they see us as different, especially when we are young and trapped in a family or school that allows for discrimination to occur. To be clear, we did not attract this. We all have different journeys and experiences in life and our thoughts and feelings do play

The Law of Attraction

a part in attracting some of our life experiences, but it is important for us to know that we do not attract the bias that we can receive from being gay.

Another reason to be aware of our own thoughts and feelings is that there are unseen Earthly energies all around us that also have an attraction to our personal energy. This is the part of energy attraction that can make some of us who are new to this idea uncomfortable, but before anyone freaks out, I do not mean ghosts, poltergeists, or demons. If anyone's mind goes there, you need to put the horror movies aside. They are made up stories for entertainment, nothing more.

The unseen energies I am referring to are thought forms created by humans, and they too can be positive or negative. Let me explain. Our human thoughts can take on an energetic existence of their own, and when we collectively focus on these thoughts, we give them more of an unseen existence. They do not have a physical form; they are more like an invisible field of energy. They can be positive or negative, but they are attracted to a person or place that matches their own vibration—the vibration they were created with. Our minds may detect these energies and interpret them as if there were a positive or negative "ghost" in our presence, but they really do not have a life, or any type of form. Thus, when we sense energies around us, we may mentally assign (visualize) a form to them, but this is a perception we are creating, it's not reality. It is just an energy that has been created by human thoughts and is now trying to find a place to exist. Most of us are not sensitive to unseen energy and don't need to worry about this, but if we are sensitive to it and don't want ego thought forms in our presence, we can clear them away just by having the intention to do so. Oh, and yes, saging (burning sage sticks or leaves) does help in clearing these energies, too.

There actually are no such things as ghosts who go clank in the night, but there are some people who can sense or feel the energy in a place or around someone that came from a past event. Along with thoughts, human actions are also energy that can leave an energetic trace, so for anyone who is sensitive to feeling the energy around themselves, they may detect the past energy of a person or event, even if it happened long ago. This past energy isn't a real tangible thing, but it too can find a home in our own energy field if it matches our vibration. If we are actively focusing our thoughts on searching for something creepy or ghostly, then we are lowering our vibe so that we can pick up on the negativity of a past event more easily. The same thing goes if we are focusing positively on detecting unseen energy, in this case we are very likely to detect or pick up on a past positive person or event.

Energies are all around us—past, present, positive and negative—but we perceive and attract the ones that match our own energy. If I ever feel negative energy around me, I will sage myself and my space and state the affirmation: "I surround myself with love and light." I am not typically a negative thinker, but sometimes I do find myself being judgmental, or maybe I have been around a person who was being toxic in their negative attitude. So just to be sure I did not take on any of this residual negative energy, I will take a moment to cleanse the energy field around my body. There are many tools we can find to help with energy clearing, but really all we need is a positive intention to clear the energy around us. Our thoughts are powerful, and they command the energy around us through the law of attraction!

Everything begins with a thought, meaning our own thoughts along with the thoughts of others set events into motion. Random thoughts come into our minds constantly, but when we choose to focus our attention on one thought specifically, we begin to give it our mental energy and allow it to expand; we put it into motion. We can see how this happens when we have a creative idea. An idea will come into our mind that inspires us, and we then choose to entertain other thoughts that help conceptualize it and bring into physical creation. For example, if an abstract artistic idea comes to our awareness, we may decide that it would be pleasurable or even profitable to create it. If so, we begin putting forth our mental energy and attracting more thoughts

The Law of Attraction

to bring it into creation. We begin to think about the colors, the canvass, the paints and even the texture. We then create a space and begin bringing it into physical existence. This is not so different from any other thoughts we focus on in our lives. When we give our attention to anything, we are giving it energy, and with enough focus, we begin attracting other energies to the thought or idea, bringing it into creation.

Most humans on Earth will never understand that we are energy and that there is an energy of attraction between everything and everyone. So of course, it does not matter whether we become aware of energy and things such as the law of attraction. But for those of us who do, life becomes next level. We become powerful when we better understand energy; we learn how to get the universe to work for us by bringing us the life that we want. We also learn how to use energy to protect ourselves and attract a happier more fulfilled life. Of course, tragedy in life will still happen because tragedy is a part of living in the physical world, but when we have a greater understanding of energy and who we truly are, we are able to overcome and handle tragedies in our lives much better. For anyone who chooses to work further with the law of attraction, you will be excited to know I am going to give more details about putting it to work in the next chapter about manifestation!

The vast majority of people are born, grow up, struggle, and go through life in misery and failure, not realizing that it would be just as easy to switch over and get exactly what they want out of life, not recognizing that the mind attracts the thing it dwells upon.
— Napoleon Hill

Spiritual Pride

"You must be the person you have never had the courage to be. Gradually, you will discover that you are that person, but until you can see this clearly, you must pretend and invent."
—Paulo Coelho

MANIFESTING

Manifesting is the process of using our thoughts and feelings to create and attract to us what we are seeking. Every creation begins with the energy of an idea or a thought, and when we apply feelings to an idea or a thought, the feelings act like a magnet to attract similar energies. Thus, when we focus on what it feels like to have what we want, we begin to carry the vibration of this feeling in our energy field, and through the law of attraction, our energy field will attract to us the things that match its vibration.

Further, when we focus on anything long enough—in this case, feeling as if we already have what we want—we program our subconscious to believe we already have it. Our subconscious mind does not know whether we truly have anything or not, so when we focus on the good feeling of already having what it is we want, we program the subconscious to believe that we do in fact have it. As a result, the subconscious becomes a powerhouse behind the scenes of our conscious awareness, automatically and continuously projecting our positive feelings of having something, which in turn attracts and manifests it. So, even if we forget to consciously manifest by focusing on the positive feeling of having something, our subconscious is still working like a magnet behind the scenes of our conscious mind to attract. Our subconscious mind translates our thoughts and feelings into energy or vibration that Spiritual Source can sense, and the subconscious in turn translates energy coming from Spiritual Source into human conscious thoughts that we can comprehend. We are always connected to and communicating with Spiritual Source energetically, whether we are consciously aware of it or not.

The subconscious mind is the mind that programs much, and in the lives of humans, it builds on an initial conscious thought.

To manifest, we begin by focusing on what it feels like to have what it is we are seeking. Some of us may have a hard time visualizing what something looks and feels like to have, and this is when a vision board becomes useful. The vision board does not do the work of creating the attraction; instead the pictures or ideas placed on the board help us to focus our mind on what our wants look and feel like. Some of us just need a reminder to visualize the positive feeling of having what it is we want, and if this is the case, a written list can be helpful—we just need to keep the list someplace where we can see it.

Another good method to help us focus on our wants is to make a recording of ourselves stating affirmations that describe how good it feels to have what we want, as if we have it already. These affirmations can be very specific, for example, "I love driving my Audi;" or more general, such as, "I am courageous, I am wealthy, I am surrounded

Manifesting

by abundance, I am at peace." We state having our wants as if we in truth already have them. The recording is also a very effective way to program our subconscious to carry the energy of having something already.

We are all different, so it doesn't matter what types of visual tools we prefer to use, or if some of us choose not to use any of them at all. If you decide to use a vision board, you can look at the photos and think about how good it feels to have what you see. If you can picture things clearly in your mind, you can visualize what you want and focus on feeling as if you already have it. It can be difficult to know what it feels like to have some things we have never had or experienced, so we can fantasize about how it feels. For example, even if we can't currently afford something we want, we can imagine we can afford it and focus on how good it feels to buy it and have it! Most important of all is to feel optimistic and think positively about yourself and your life. When you focus on feeling positive, you attract more positive outcomes for yourself.

Within all of us is a divine capacity to manifest and attract all that we need and desire — *Wayne Dyer*

Instructions for manifesting

To begin with, think about what it is that you want in your life. Think big, do not limit yourself—if you want it, then you deserve it! Take the wants that resonate with you and write them out on a list. If you want to also make a recording of yourself affirming what you want, and how it feels to have it, then do that as well. If you like the idea of creating a vision board, then by all means find images, words and items that represent what you want and affix them to it. You could do all three of these things if you so desire, or you can just visualize what you want in your head and focus on how it feels. Whatever you decide to do, be creative and make the process fun and inspiring. The more creative you are with manifesting, the more interested you will be in keeping up with the process.

Next, focus on how it feels to have what you want. The more you feel the positive feelings of already having it, the more you carry the vibration of having it subconsciously, which will work continuously to attract it. Do whatever you need to do to help keep you focused on feeling good and in positive alignment with what you are seeking. Thoughts create, feelings attract—use your thoughts to think about what you want and put your feelings to work in attracting it. *It's important that the feelings we focus on are positive feelings of having it, and not based on the thoughts of not having what we want. If we keep reminding ourselves of how we feel lack or disappointment by not having something in our life, we are not creating a positive attraction.*

If you are trying to manifest a relationship, focus on how good it feels to spend time with someone and share your life with them. Money and relationships do not just show up in your bank account or on your doorstep; you will still have to get yourself out in life and find the paths being created by the universe that lead you to these opportunities. But, when you focus on your feelings and wants, the paths to getting you what you seek become more numerous and prevalent. You

Manifesting

will begin to notice synchronicities such as events and people coming into your life that help get you to what you are seeking.

When you awake in the morning, set the stage of your day by focusing on having a beautiful and enjoyable day. If some days you find that it's difficult to do this, then focus on what you are grateful for in your life or state your positive affirmations. The goal here is to keep your mindset in a positive vibration to attract more positive events into your life. We should not entertain bad thoughts and expect someone or something to come along and change how we feel. This makes us dependent upon other people and things outside ourselves to make us feel better—something that can be unreliable.

Throughout your day, take moments to think positive thoughts about yourself and what you want. The key to manifesting is being diligent about feeling that you have what you seek already. If you forget to focus on that feeling for a few days, do not give up. Get back to focusing on feeling good about what it is you are seeking. Once you have sufficiently programmed your subconscious mind, it will work behind the scenes of your awareness to bring to you what you seek–even when you forget to focus.

Enjoy the process of manifesting, believe in your worthiness and your ability to attract. The only thing that stands in your way is the doubt of your own ego mind. Stay in positive alignment with Spiritual Source and focus on how good it feels to have what you want. You got this!

A note on wants

It's important to take note of whether we want something to enjoy in our life, or whether we want it to make us feel better. If our happiness depends on getting something we want, we may find that once we have it, it does not really change how we feel, even if it brings us a temporary feel-good high. For example, if we expect that having a luxury car will make us feel better about ourselves, we may be disappointed when we eventually get the car but we still feel the same. When we focus on wanting things so that they can help our self-esteem or change our ego thinking, it is very likely they will do neither. Self-esteem starts from loving ourselves, not getting attention from others because of what we own. Thus, when we focus on wanting material things, we should want them because having them brings us joy; we should not want them because we are unhappy, and we expect them to change how we feel. True joy begins within ourselves and feeling joyful is what helps to attract more of the positive things we want.

I have known many people (including myself) who thought that once they had a certain material thing they would feel happiness and fulfillment, but the excitement was only temporary. It's not hard to fall into the belief that material things will make us feel better and be a better person, because most of us grow up in a consumer and materialistic culture—a culture that leads us to believe that if we have a beautiful body, own nice things or carry the right title, then we will be loved and accepted. But, if we use our looks or what we own to define who we are, then these things may attract people who want to possess us as a good-looking trophy or who want to be with us because of what we own. These types of superficial relationships don't help us to be authentic and they may lead us to feeling not-so-great about ourselves—perhaps even feeling used.

As for living in a consumer culture, I am sure many of us have fallen into feeling the constant need to buy new things. This is because we are not taught how to feel personally fulfilled with ourselves. Instead we are taught how to want more. As a result, many of us are walking around with a big energetic void that we are seeking to have filled by something or someone. When we are wrapped up in ego and consumerism, we tend to forget who we really are, and how it's the little things that happen daily in our lives that bring us true fulfilment and joy. Instead of learning to love ourselves, we continue to shop and buy new

Manifesting

clothes, cars, phones, cosmetics and gadgets, all in the hope they will make us feel better.

There is a thrill in buying new things, but once the high of getting something new wears off, we are quickly back to searching for the next thing to buy. This cycle of wanting is not accidental. It is perfectly orchestrated and programmed into our minds by the marketing geniuses of our world. They master images and stories to make us want what they have to offer, and they are very effective in their campaigns. We are programmed to prize having things and to portray who we are through our looks and the things we own, but it can lead to a lack of knowledge about who we truly are. True fulfillment and contentment in our lives is something that we discover for ourselves in our daily routine and experiences; our consumer culture will not teach us how to feel true fulfilment through their ads and commercials.

I could go on about the various things we may choose to focus our attention on and whether they will actually make us feel how we hoped they would. It's important to take note of the way some of our desires are a result of being programmed to think we need them to feel better or to be accepted. It's best to want things because they add to our joy in living. There is absolutely nothing wrong with manifesting an AMG Mercedes because it is fast and thrilling to drive, but we shouldn't want it because it will attract someone who wants to be with us because of what we have.

We really need to focus on being authentic with ourselves and surrounding ourselves with other authentic people. There are some really good actors out there who will notice those of us who show off our things, and they will indeed seek us out. Unfortunately, if we are not realistic and authentic with ourselves, we may fall easily into another person's agenda and a phony relationship—a relationship where someone seeks what they can get out of us and does not care one bit about who we truly are.

All knowing Spiritual Source

Spiritual Source always knows what is best for us because it senses the energy around us along with everything else that exists; it always sees the bigger picture. When we want something, Spiritual Source knows how it will energetically fit into our lives and also what it will lead to. We have free will to think and create as we choose and if we want something that is in alignment with our greater good, Spiritual Source will work to bring it into our existence. Even if what we want is not in our true best interest, but we believe it is, Spiritual Source will still work to bring it to us because we have free will to manifest as we choose. But, because Spiritual Source understands the patterns of energy leading to the manifestation as well as the events that can happen as a result of it, Spiritual Source knows if our desire is not truly in our own best interest. If it isn't, Spiritual Source works to bring us what we seek, but will also present to us better options or paths that we may choose instead.

When focusing on what we want, sometimes we make wrong choices. We may think we really want or need something, but we just can't see that it's not the best thing for us. I'm sure we have all wanted something in our lives, perhaps we were at one time even obsessed with getting it, and then we either got it and had buyer's remorse or we were never able to achieve having it. But, then something better came along and when we went with the better option we looked back and thought, "What was I thinking wanting something else in the first place? I am so glad I chose the path I took instead."

There are many paths we can take in life, but Spiritual Source is always helping to create the best path for us. If we are manifesting something but are not sure if it's in our best interest, Spiritual Source will also bring something that is in alignment with what we are seeking, but better. Our journey in life is discovering what we want to experience and going with the best option.

MEDITATION AND MINDFULNESS

"Meditation is not a way of making the mind go quiet. It's a way of entering into the quiet that's already there—buried under the 50,000 thoughts the average person thinks every day."
—Deepak Chopra

Meditation and mindfulness are both tools to help bring us into the present moment and experience a peaceful state of awareness. Being in a peaceful state of awareness is our natural state of being; it's what we experience in our youth before we are led to focus on our ego thinking, or begin living in our heads. By having a meditation or mindfulness practice, we become grounded and centered, or in other words, we feel at ease and a sense of peace. Everything begins to feel all right in our lives and we become focused on what really matters.

Meditation

I have talked to many people who have expressed an interest in meditation but have felt as though they couldn't do it because they could not quiet their thoughts. The first thing I try to help them understand is that constant thoughts are normal for all of us. Second, the purpose of learning meditation isn't to stop our thoughts; instead it's a process of learning how to stop focusing our awareness on them. It may take patience and practice, but we can absolutely learn how to move our awareness beyond our thoughts. And, when we discover how to do this, we will experience a sense of peace that is very beneficial to our mind, body and spiritual connection. Because of these great benefits to meditation, we should not allow our relentless thoughts to deter us from trying it; our thoughts are expected to happen.

One of the great benefits of practicing meditation is that it strengthens the skill of being able to control what we think about throughout our day. At any given moment, we can switch our thoughts from those that are troublesome or stressful to thoughts that are peaceful. We become less reactionary and less provoked by the actions and words of other people, and if we do become upset, we know how to quickly switch focus back to a calm state of awareness. Through meditation, we learn that we are not victims of our thoughts, or the thoughts and ideas projected onto us by others. If we don't like the idea that someone is trying to put into our minds, we can automatically switch the thought off simply by moving our awareness away from it.

We should be in control of our thoughts and emotions, they should not control us. If anyone feels they cannot control what they think about or how they feel, then I highly recommend starting a meditation practice. When we learn how to turn our conscious awareness away from our thoughts, we bring our mind and body into a truly relaxed state, helping to calm our digestion, breathing, heart rate and even blood pressure.

Meditation and Mindfulness

We also allow for a greater connection to our Spirit because our resistant ego thoughts are no longer blocking our connection. This allows us to be in the "flow" of receiving physical, emotional, and mental well-being along with intuitive insight and wisdom. We are always connected to the energy of our Spirit, it does not come and go. Through mediation we simply get our ego out of the way and allow ourselves to receive the stream of well-being that is always flowing to us.

One of the most interesting things we will discover by meditating is that we are not our thoughts. The analyzing, judging, worrying, the need to do this or that—this is not who we truly are. All of these things are the result of our ego minds applying our own personal filter to the experiences of life, leading us to obsess and stress over life's little details. The ego mind is what we learn, it's the filter through which we think or analyze our experience, but beyond this learned filter, we exist in a peaceful and loving state of awareness. A state of awareness that quietly observes life in non-judgement is our natural state of being.

Meditation is an important part of my everyday routine and it helps to keep my husband and me grounded and emotionally balanced in our busy lives. The person who taught me how to meditate would get up in the morning, brush his teeth and then sit upright in his bed to meditate, and this worked just great for him and his wife. I have meditated on airplanes and I used to do a quick meditation in front of my computer when I worked in a corporate environment. Meditating at work helped me to clear my mind and increase my ability to focus, which I needed for the legal work I was doing at that time. I do make use of earphones to play meditation music when I am in public and if anyone has a lot of activity going on at home, this can help there too. We need to avoid listening to our favorite dance music and pop artists before meditating because this music is like mental crack and we will find ourselves singing the song over and over in our heads, thus making it much harder for us to ignore our thoughts. Instead, I recommend playing binaural beats, spa music/meditation music or white noise—there is plenty of

Spiritual Pride

this type of music found on YouTube.

Meditation is something we can learn to do anywhere, but I prefer to be in a space that offers a sense of tranquility and little noise distraction. Some people have mastered meditating in a noisy and busy space without earplugs or headphones, but I am not one of those people—I am easily distracted by sound and movement. My husband and I are fortunate that we have an extra room in our house that we were able to designate just for meditating. Not only does this room provide us a peaceful place to meditate, it is also a room for being mindful of being loved, for gratitude and for relaxation. We also use this room to do energy work such as reiki, which helps to balance and heal our energy. We have put things in this room that inspire us to relax and feel good, such as special gifts from friends, art and many types of crystals.

Before my father passed away, he learned that I liked rocks and crystals, so he spent the last part of his life traveling the western United States to find them. He found many beautiful stones and crystals, laying in the dirt or covered in mud, which he would take home. He then cleaned off the mud by hand and bought stone cutters and polishers to turn what most of us would overlook in nature into beautiful cut stones and crystal clusters. I feel blessed to have had such a gift from my father—he put a lot of time and effort in bringing me something he knew would bring me joy. Many of these beautiful stones and crystals are on display in our meditation room and they add a natural and calming feeling to the space.

What goes into a meditation space is up to each of us, but a fountain, comfortable chairs, ambient lighting, pillows, an essential oil diffuser and art work are all wonderful things to put in a meditation room. Some people do not want anything in a meditation room to distract them, and that is perfectly fine as well.

I realize that many of us do not have a spare room to create this type of space, and money can be an issue in buying furnishings, but none of these things are needed to meditate. Things just help some of us feel as if we are stepping into a different atmosphere that allows us to separate ourselves from the thoughts and events of our day. Instead of a designated room, you could just as easily find a comfortable spot on a sofa, put some headphones on if there is background noise and even hold a crystal if it feels good to do that. Nature is also an excellent place to meditate. Focusing on the sounds of birds, moving water or the breeze though the grasses and trees can be conducive to meditation.

How to meditate

I do not define the type of meditation I do, but if I needed to define it, I would probably call it spiritual meditation. Spiritual meditation is the process of moving our focus away from the outer world and bringing it inward to connect to our Spirit, which is what I do in meditation. I will offer instruction on how I meditate, but there is no one correct way of doing it. If my method does not feel right for you, do some research and find what resonates with you.

Once you have found a space to sit comfortably and quietly, you can prepare yourself to meditate by taking long deep breaths. By taking a deep breath in, and then slowly breathing it out, you relax the body and ease physical tension. To help with relaxation, you can visualize along with your breathing that calming and healing energy comes into you with the inhalation and negativity and stress leave with the exhalation. You are powerful in your intentions, so if you believe that this works, then it does and so it will!

While deep breathing, focus on any parts of your body that may feel tight and bring your attention to relaxing the muscles in that area. It may take a few minutes to scan your entire body and relax each part of yourself and that is OK. Take as much time as you need. Once you find yourself physically relaxed, you can bring your breathing back to a normal and comfortable pace.

Spiritual Pride

It's important to not worry about time, so if you are on a schedule, you can set a timer for the amount of time you wish to meditate. This will allow you the freedom of not having to keep a scheduled time on your mind. When first learning to meditate, try doing it for a few minutes, gradually working toward going longer. It does not have to take long to receive the benefits of meditating, but I usually meditate for twenty to thirty minutes because I find that is what works best for me. Do not worry about how long it takes, do what works best for you. Even if it's just a few minutes, it is still beneficial.

The first thing you will notice when you close your eyes and sit in silence is that your thoughts are there, and they may keep coming. Do not worry about trying to control them or fear that you can't stop them. Your focus is not on stopping your thoughts; rather it's on not giving them your attention. So, when a thought comes into your mind, ignore it, do not focus your attention on it. You will of course recognize the thought, but you are not feeding it the energy it needs to expand in your mind. The thought cannot persist without your attention; it will dissipate. By continuing the practice of ignoring your thoughts, they will eventually stop coming into your awareness.

This process may at first feel relentless, but with practice you will be able to sit quietly and not entertain any thoughts at all. When this happens, you slip into a peaceful state of awareness that is difficult to describe. You are awake, but you enter into a tranquil non-thinking state—it's a blissful feeling. After meditating it can feel as if you are awakening but you were never asleep. You will feel rejuvenated, inspired, and experience a deep sense of peace. I feel tingles going up and down my spine, and this tells me that I connected fully with my Spirit.

Meditating can indeed seem difficult at first, but it is only difficult because we are taught to believe we always need to be thinking. If anyone feels they are different because their minds are constantly bombarded with thoughts, they are not! This is why, in some types of meditation, a mantra is used to help. A mantra is just a nonsensical word or phrase we use to focus our attention instead of trying to focus on no thought at all.

If you want to try a mantra you can look for examples online or even can create your own. For example, you could use the word "peace" as a mantra. Thus, whenever a thought comes into your mind during your meditation, you move your attention from the thought by focusing on the word peace instead. You are not focusing on what the word peace means, you are just focusing on saying the word as a distraction to keep you from focusing your attention on your thoughts. If the word peace triggers you to think, then find a word to repeat that is nonsensical.

It does not matter if we have to practically chant our chosen mantra. It is a mind training tool, and eventually it becomes easier not to focus on our thoughts. Eventually, we will find ourselves in a blissful, quiet and peaceful state of mind, not needing to say a mantra at all.

When we meditate, our attention moves inward, and this allows us to connect more fully to the peace and love of Spiritual Source. It is through this enhanced connection that we receive a balancing of our energy along with inspiring thoughts and ideas. Energies coming from Source are downloaded into our subconscious, which then translates this energy into wisdom and inspiration for our conscious mind. This translated inspiration and wisdom will come into our conscious awareness either right after meditating or when a relevant thought triggers it. If we think we are getting inspiration while we are meditating, we should ignore it and continue focusing on non-thought or our mantra. The information will come back to us later as needed.

Meditation is a practice and it can take some time to master, but please do not get discouraged. Eventually you will find yourself sitting in a peaceful and quiet state of awareness without a barrage of thoughts coming into your mind. When you are done meditating, your thoughts will come back, but you will feel refreshed, rejuvenated and your thoughts will be peaceful. This brings us into a healthier and more balanced state of mind, allowing us to perform even better throughout our day. If we are meditating at the end of the day, it allows for the stress and distraction of the day to dissipate, helping us to physically relax.

I have presented what works for me, but I realize sometimes meditation is best taught in person by an instructor. You may be able to find a meditation instructor in your area or you can find video tutorials online. If you like my method of meditation and need further assistance, I am happy to help! I offer instruction that can be done over skype or zoom, which you can schedule on my website transcendentlifestyle.

Mindfulness

I realize meditation is not for everyone. Some people simply do not like the idea of sitting in silence despite the many benefits of doing so. And, this is OK! We are all unique in our preferences. It may be better for someone to take a yoga class where they focus quietly on movement, or take a walk in nature where they observe a non-ego environment. We can also sit with ourselves and just focus our attention on our connection to Spiritual Source and how this connection feels. Mindfulness encompasses all of these things, but it can also just be feeling thankful or having gratitude for what we have in our lives.

Mindfulness is something I do daily in addition to meditation. I enjoy quietly observing the nature around my house, showing gratitude for what I have in my life and also sometimes doing energy healing through reiki and qigong. There are many other things I do that allow me to have mindful moments, such as appreciating art work, hiking, kayaking, creating abstract paintings and making semi-precious gemstone bracelets. All of these bring me into a peaceful state of presence. The technique or activity is not what is important; what is important is being in the present moment, taking our focus off of our ego thoughts and observing or doing something through peaceful awareness.

Ideas for Mindfulness

There is plenty of information online to get ideas and even instructions on being mindful. Any of us can do a little research and choose some techniques that resonate with us. Or, we can just enjoy the journey by discovering our own ways to bring peace of mind into our lives. The following are some ideas to help get you started:

- Write a list of things that you are thankful for in your life. Feel the good feelings of being grateful; it helps to bring peace and happiness to your mind.

- Sit peacefully and observe nature or art, or listen to classical or meditation music. Orchestral music is very soothing and inspirational; it tells a non-verbal story to the mind.

- Try yoga, qigong, tai chi or any other type of focused body movement

- Learn how to do energy healing work such as reiki.

- Hiking, walking, gardening, kayaking—any relaxing outdoor activity—brings us into a peaceful awareness just by being in nature. Nature exists in a non-ego and non-judgmental state that allows us to feel accepted and part of something bigger. Gardening provides us a sense of purpose and it is rewarding to see how our efforts in planting lead to growth, followed by harvest and blooms.

- And of course, stop to smell the roses. It feels good to notice the beauty in the little things that cross our daily paths.

Mindfulness isn't difficult, we just need to remember to do it. —Sharon Salzberg

INTUITION

With a better understanding of how our bodies can sense energy, it should be no surprise that we are able to receive from Spiritual Source an inner knowing or guidance known as intuition. Intuition comes to us as an energy frequency that our bodies detect or feel; it does not come to us through spoken words or outward images. Once energy coming from Spiritual Source is detected by our body, our subconscious mind translates this energy to conscious thoughts that we can make sense of. How we interpret intuitive energy is up to each of us, but it comes from our inner Soul connection, not from energies outside ourselves. We are all unique in how we perceive this energy, so some of us may interpret it as images/visions or words that come into our minds, but mostly it comes to us as a gut feeling.

Spiritual Pride

Spiritual Source is always communicating to us through energy because we are always connected to Spiritual Source via our Soul. It is up to our own conscious minds as to whether or not we pay attention to the insight this connection brings to us, but it's in our best interest to pay attention. Spiritual Source knows what the energy of our actions and decisions can lead to—something we cannot always see from our limited human perspectives.

There are many examples of how and why we receive intuitive feelings. For instance, intuitive guidance can be perceived as a gut feeling to either go somewhere or stay away from a certain place. Maybe it's a strong urge to be around a certain person, or to avoid them. It can even be the urge to do something nice for someone by paying them a compliment. Spiritual Source knows when someone could really use some kind words.

Guidance can come to us as a sudden craving to eat or drink something that helps to balance our bodies, or we can have a gut feeling about a new job, relationship or a creative idea. There are just so many reasons why we receive this gentle and loving guidance that comes to us from Spiritual Source. We don't need to define specifically how it happens, we can just focus on allowing it to come to us and it will, in a manner that is best suited for each of us.

The area of our body where the energy of intuition is received is in our gut area, which is the seat of our solar plexus chakra. It is not important to have a full understanding of the chakra systems, but they are energy centers in our body that relate to various energetic functions. Thus, one of the functions of the solar plexus chakra is being a transmitter. It receives energetic insight while also projecting the energy of our feelings to Spiritual Source. *Because of this, the solar plexus chakra plays a role in the process of manifesting because it's projecting our feelings of having.* When intuitive energy is received by the solar plexus energy center, it is then translated by the subconscious from a gut feeling into conscious thoughts that we can analyze. Thus, when intuitive feelings come to us, we can mentally put two and two together to come to a conclusion about what we are doing or about to do and the intuitive physical feelings we are receiving about it.

Intuition is different from psychic insight because psychic insight comes from outside ourselves while intuition comes from within us. To be psychic is to have the ability to use our bodies as an antenna to detect the energies surrounding ourselves and other people. An experienced psychic can read the ego energies around a person and some can even detect the residual ego of a deceased person. The energy of a deceased person is not a ghost or spirit, Spirit always reunites fully with Spiritual Source. Instead, what is detected is the ego energy and personality of a deceased person that a living person keeps in their own field of energy. That is, we can hold onto the memory of loved ones, and in doing so we keep a part of their energy alive in our presence. This is a beautiful thing, in a way, it makes us feel as if they are still with us. Eventually, in time, the ego energy of a deceased person will dissipate, especially when we choose to no longer hold onto their memory. If the ego energy of a deceased person does not feel good to us, we can choose to release it. Doing energy clearing such as saging will help in the process of releasing; saging helps to focus our intention on clearing or releasing energy.

A psychic may be born with an enhanced ability to interpret outside energy through a vision or even by hearing words, but it is a skill most of us will not experience, although we can work on developing it. We are all somewhat psychic, because we all have the ability to sense the unseen energy around us on some level. It's just that many of us are not born to do it or we do not try to develop it. It is not common for most of us to be taught how to recognize our sixth sense or even believe in it, but some of us do not want to enhance this ability because it can lead us to being very sensitive. The ego energies of the human collective can be very unsettled and because of this, some of us don't

Spiritual Pride

want to feel the hateful and fearful energy coming from and surrounding other people.

If anyone wants to enhance psychic abilities I suggest you learn from a teacher because you will want to learn how to be in control of when you want to use it versus when you do not! You will pick up on both the good and bad energy that is all around the human collective—something we don't always want to feel. Developing our intuition is always in our best interest because it always comes to us from a positive and loving stream of energy that serves our greatest good, so we never have to worry about negativity coming from Spiritual Source.

We are all intuitive, but many of us do not pay attention to it because we are taught to pay attention to our ego thoughts alone. Our ego thoughts tend to focus on what others say, and our analysis of what has happened or what may happen. Because intuition does not come to us through the ego mind directly, our ego may actually block us from recognizing it. It does this by choosing to overlook it or by putting its own spin on what the insight means, leading us away from it. It's also likely the ego will create a disbelief in our ability to receive intuitive insight because the ego is not part of the process, it is not part of our Spirit. Intuition is based on our connection to Spiritual Source, while our ego helps to create the feeling of being separate from it.

I will give an example to help explain how our ego minds may overlook or ignore intuition. I have learned through trial and error that if my stomach starts to feel unsettled or I feel anxious before going someplace, going there is not going to be in my best interest. It will be a waste of my time or a bad experience. Of course, I have ignored such intuitive feelings many times, which is the reason I know my intuition was trying to tell me something! I felt an unsettled sensation in my gut prior to going somewhere, but my ego mind wanted to continue pursuing what I was doing, so I chose to overlook my intuition and go anyway. Each time I did this, I discovered it was a mistake not to listen to what my gut feeling was trying to tell me. I would say to myself

Intuition

afterwards, "You knew, but you didn't listen. You went ahead and did it anyway!"

I do pay attention to these gut feelings now, but unfortunately sometimes if I made a commitment to go somewhere, I may need to honor the commitment. In this case, I fully recognize the gut feelings I am receiving regarding the commitment and mentally prepare myself to be resilient or think of a way I can limit the experience—I better prepare myself for what is to come.

There are those who think they have to do some type of ritual work or other activity to activate intuition. For instance, I have heard of people thinking they need to be on a certain diet, do psychic exercises or be in a spiritual place like Sedona, Arizona.

It's OK for us to have our own truths about this process, but none of these things are needed for intuition. All we really have to do is learn how to move our awareness beyond our ego thoughts and pay attention to the feelings we get. An exercise we can do to move beyond our ego thoughts and focus on expanding our intuition is to imagine our solar plexus chakra expanding. The solar plexus chakra is centered in our gut area, and it's the reason for feeling a "gut instinct." The color associated with the solar plexus chakra is yellow, so to help with imagining, you can visualize a yellow sphere of energy expanding in your gut area. See it as vibrant, healthy and radiating out of you. Just by focusing your attention on it, you are working to expand it. While doing this, you can also ask for intuitive guidance if you desire, or you can just feel how good it feels to have something you want (manifesting). *Guidance does not typically come right away, but in time it does come to us as an insight or an a-ha moment.*

It's best for all of us to listen to our intuition, and for us gays, it can help guide us to be safe and healthy in a sometimes mean and hateful world. We should listen to unexplained feelings or anxiety about doing something. For example, if we are thinking about walking to a local bar or restaurant but we suddenly have an unexplained bad feeling come to us about it, we should pay attention to this feeling. Even if it feels irrational to our ego minds, we should consider at least taking a different route or better yet, getting a driver.

It helps to pay attention to our intuition when we meet new people because this too can be very beneficial to our safety and well-being. Many people act in ways that are not representative of their true intentions, but our intuition can help us to see through their facade by giving us a sense of their real intentions. If we are out and about and we meet someone, we should be protective of ourselves if our intuition is telling us they are not who they are portraying themselves to be. With the help of our intuition, we are better able to detect the proverbial wolf in sheep's clothing. We don't need to create drama by calling someone out over an intuitive feeling, we can just walk away. People with hidden agendas do not want to be exposed and if you try to expose them, you may get to witness their true colors—something you may not want to experience.

It's good to remember that a hunch about someone comes from our intuition, but we can also feel the vibes coming from other people and places too. I am sure we all have experienced the feeling of someone staring at us only to turn and find out that indeed they were. Of course, this is different from intuition; this is feeling another person's vibe or psychic energy, and in these situations, we can typically sense their intention, but if we are unsure of their intention, then we can rely on our intuition.

For anyone wishing to better understand intuition versus ego thoughts, learn how to follow the source of the thought or feeling. For example, let's say you are thinking about an upcoming party. If you are worried you are not going to fit in or look good enough, these are ego insecurities, which are making you feel anxious. If you expect to have a good time or you're not really analyzing how you think the party will be, yet you have an anxious or unsettled gut feeling associated with the

Intuition

idea of going to the party, then this could be your intuition letting you know you may not want to go.

The next time you ignore an uneasy feeling that does not seem to be related to anything you currently know about a situation, pay attention to the outcome of the situation. This is one way to learn to recognize our unique methods for receiving intuition, and also how to strengthen it by giving it more of our attention. But, please be safe. If you get a strong intuitive feeling not to go somewhere or do something, please have faith in the power of your intuition and follow the advice of these feelings—it can be the guidance that saves your life.

Paying attention to the subtle intuitive cues we receive can help lead us to a successful path in life while avoiding things that could be detrimental to us. We are all different in how we perceive energy, so take some time to discover what your unique way of receiving intuition feels like. It is in your best interest to allow your intuitive connection because it is always working for your greatest good!

"You are a limitless being. Your divinity makes you limitless. The Source lies within you. Your intuition is when the Source is speaking through you."
—Sanchita Pandey

CONNECTING TO SPIRITUAL SOURCE

On the ultimate level, our human experience, our Spirit and our Soul connection, are one in the same. Our Spirit exists in a non-physical state that is connected to everything else that makes up Spiritual Source, but our Spirit simultaneously has the experience of separation through being human. Separation is ultimately an illusion, but the human ego mind and physical body allow for our Spirit to experience what it feels like to exist as an individual person with a limited perception.

It can be difficult to see beyond the belief that our human experience, our Spirit and the Source of everything (God), are all separate buckets because this is what we are taught through religion. This belief leads us to look outside ourselves to connect to our greater Spirit or God because we believe they are separate from us humans. We also tend to believe they are superior to us, but the truth is, they are us, we are them, we are not separate—we are our Spirit having a human experience. Connecting to Spiritual Source does not bring us back together because we already exist together; instead it's the process of moving our awareness beyond the belief of separation and focusing on the connection that exists within each one of us.

Awakening is the process of becoming aware of our ego mind and being able to see beyond it. It is discovering who and what we truly are—Spirit.

It may help to use the concept of realms when describing our human connection to Spiritual Source, but we must realize that one realm is not better than another. All realms are ultimately connected and make up one universal consciousness. Our non-physical Spirits are in a higher realm of existence, and collectively they make up Spiritual Source. Higher refers to all knowing, not better than. Thus, the greater non-physical part of our Spirit exists in a higher realm because it is all knowing and recognizes its connection to every other Spirit and all of creation. Spirit exists in a state of connectedness to all other Spirits, but they have the experience of separateness by being human. Because of this ability, our Spirit can exist in higher realms and lower realms at the same time—lower just meaning a limited perception that allows for the experience of believing we are separate. We do not have to understand how this is possible. All we need to know is that Spirit exists in a state of all knowing and loving bliss in higher realms while also experiencing the influence of the lower realms of human ego mind, an experience that can allow for both negative and positive experiences. Spirit chooses to have this experience; it is not a test or a mission, but our Spirit does grow and expand from the experience.

Energy coming from Spiritual Source is behind all of physical creation and it works through the laws of nature to create the physical body that is needed for Spirit to inhabit. Spirit does not just inhabit human bodies. It also inhabits animals, plants and trees—anything that has an experience has Spirit inhabiting it. But the level of conscious awareness will vary depending on the species. Humans are unique in that we are created with the ability to have an awareness of our greater reality, but because of our ego mind, it can become difficult to awaken to it. This leads most people to sleepwalk through life. Because of this, humans will co-exist together, yet exist in very different mental realms.

The ability to exist on many different mental realms will lead us to have perceptions and life experiences that can differ greatly from one another. Becoming aware of our spiritual connection and existing in a higher realm will not bring us some type of greater afterlife reward. Being rewarded or punished in an afterlife is simply an idea created by humans. Those who exist in a closed minded or unaware state of mind while on Earth are still equally loved—they too are part of divine Spirit. Spirit wishes to have all types of experiences and it does not need us to mentally awaken in this lifetime to go back home; we all go back home equally.

However, existing in a higher mental realm does allow us to have a more rewarding life experience. In a higher mental realm, we discover that we have the freedom to live our lives more fully and authentically; we know that we came here to follow our hearts' desires and not to reach some type of human perfection. We become aware of how ego is the only creator of fear, judgement, insecurity, uncertainty and animosity. With this recognition, we learn to free our minds from the mental chains of ego, leading us to feel more at peace with ourselves and others. We also have a greater reverence for nature and the lives inhabiting it because we understand that they too are an aspect of Spirit having an experience—all of Earth's creations are divine and deserve respect.

The majority of us are not born into families or cultures that will teach us how to recognize, or awaken to, our greater spiritual reality.

Spiritual Pride

Instead, many of us will sense something greater within ourselves, which will inspire us to begin a journey of truth seeking. Our spiritual journeys will be unique, but as we begin the process of awakening to our greater reality, we may need to address some common mental blocks that stand in our way. Mental blocks are caused by the filters of our ego mind, so depending on our unique education and experiences, we may or may not have them. However, if we discover that we have any of the following mental blocks, it is best for us to address them, and then let them go. Doing so will allow us to further awaken and get ourselves into a greater alignment with Spiritual Source.

One of the most common blocks to our awakening process is our tendency to complicate spirituality. For example, some believe they must go to a church or sanctuary to be closer to God, or do rituals and say specific prayers to a deity or messiah. These things make sense to some, and that is perfectly OK, but we do not need to do any of these things to expand our spiritual awareness or our connection to Spirit. Connecting to Spiritual Source is really as simple as quieting our minds and enjoying a moment of peace. When we are in a peaceful state of awareness, we get our ego out of the way and we share our thoughts with Spiritual Source, which feels the energy of our intention. If we are associating positive, high vibrational feelings to our intention, Spiritual Source will know to assist in whatever it is that we are seeking, whether guidance, wisdom or something else that we want.

Another block to the process of awakening and connecting more fully to our Spirit is feeling that we are unworthy. Nothing stands in our way of expanding our connection to Spiritual Source except our own feelings of being less than. We are all absolutely worthy of this connection, but it can be difficult for some of us to get past the ingrained belief that we are inferior. Anyone who has grown up in a religious culture has likely been mentally programmed to believe in a God who is superior to us and through its superiority, it judges us and is critical of our actions.

Connecting to Spiritual Source

Less awakened people may even fear for their lives and afterlives if they dare question what they have been told to believe, leading them to feel more comfortable having someone speak to a God on their behalf. If anyone feels this way, they need to realize we are not separate from Spiritual Source, we are the product of Spirit's choice to have a physical experience. It was never meant to be perfect, devout or a test. We have a divine right to be true to ourselves and the free will to connect to our spiritual home anytime we want. We do not need anyone to do this for us; we are all worthy of our own divine connection.

Disbelief is one of the trickiest blocks to connecting more fully to Spiritual Source. There are those who have been so turned off by the belief of a judgmental God and the dogma imposed by religions, that they choose to believe in nothing at all and would need proof to see beyond their own disbelief. Proof is given to those who open their minds and ask to receive it, but Spiritual Source does not interfere with our free will to be on a chosen journey of non-belief. Thus, if we refuse to believe until proof shows up for us, it likely never will—one must ask to receive.

Spiritual Source does not think with a human mind, so it does not feel offended when we chose not to recognize it. It also does not feel the need to push proof of its existence upon us because it allows us to experience this life in the realm of our choosing. If non-belief becomes a detriment to our life experience, it is not a decision made by Spiritual Source to punish us; rather it is from our own free will to diminish the connection and the sense of well-being that can come with it. All of us are divine and equally loved whether we believe in a higher power or not.

Some of you may be wondering how receiving anything from Spiritual Source is even possible. I get it—we are human, and we see life as solid, so yes it can seem strange or impossible to receive healing, protection and knowledge from something that is non-physical. In the beginning it may take an act of faith, but there are indeed powerful spiritual energies that respond to our positive intentions. They can perform what we humans would call miracles. It is up to us to believe or not, but our experiences will match what we choose: If you don't believe, miracles may not happen for you. Believe, and they will!

You are the creator of your experience and you have free will to receive assistance or ignore it and close yourself off from it. You are not judged by Spiritual Source no matter what you choose, but if you want help, the greater non-physical part of ourselves wants nothing more than to assist.

When I first began my spiritual journey, I did not believe I could connect to Spiritual Source on my own. I believed I needed a psychic medium to do this for me, and it took going to psychics in the beginning to develop a faith in something beyond our physical lives. The mediums were successful in providing me the confirmation I was seeking, and I became more comfortable with the idea that there is a non-physical existence all around us that we can call home. In time, I became even more curious and decided to go to a metaphysical university to get a more in-depth understanding of spirituality.

This education led me to a greater understanding of being connected to Spiritual Source and it also gave me more confidence to ask Source directly for answers. Soon after I began to ask, I was intuitively guided to allow Source to come into my mind and inspire my writing. Because of this connection, much of what I write is inspired through my own ability to receive wisdom from Spiritual Source.

Expanding my connection to Spiritual Source has been an amazing and life changing journey for me, and it would never have happened if I did not have the intention to connect and get answers. Along with wisdom, I have received a sense of well-being, abundance and security that I have never before felt in my life. I feel uplifted and comfortable in my own skin. Opening myself to having a connection to Source has also given me the courage to step out of my comfort zone and share my experiences with others.

> *"There are only two ways to live your life. One is as though nothing is a miracle. The other is as though everything is a miracle." —Albert Einstein*

Our interpretations of how heavenly realms exist or what they look like will differ—this is just part of the individual human journey. We do not need to worry whether our view is right or wrong because Spiritual Source is ultimately energy, and how this energy looks or acts is up to our own interpretation. What is important is that we feel good about our chosen way to perceive because it's through our own filters that we will experience our unique connection. With that said, if the beliefs you are comfortable with consist of angels or fairies or perhaps Jesus, Buddha, or Krishna, you can use these as the visual or mental ambassadors to represent your spiritual connection. If none of these things appeal to you and you are more comfortable with the idea of non-physical looking like pure white light energy, or looking like nothing at all, it is all fine. It does not matter to Spiritual Source what you call it or what you think it looks like; it feels your intention to connect and it feels what you are seeking.

Personally, I have always liked the idea of having guides that I consider to be beings of light or energy that exist to help us. Having a guide or even believing they exist is not something any of us must do; it is just a concept I feel comfortable with because it helps me to assign a meaning and a name to something I cannot fully comprehend. Having a guide helps me focus my intention, and I like to call upon my guide for assistance with many different things. I ask my guide to protect me, my home, my car when I'm driving, and also to protect my loved ones. I ask my guide to give me insight into my writings and assist in bringing me what I am actively trying to manifest. I also ask my guide to show me the best routes in life, along with assisting me in healing.

Ways to connect to Spiritual Source

All of our journeys are unique, so of course my way of connecting is not the only way. If my method resonates with you, then it's an honor for me to be able to inspire you, but if it does not, that's perfectly OK. Perhaps you already have a preferred method, or you want to develop your own. What is important is that you know that you are always loved by Spiritual Source and it is your intention that allows you to contact home. You are divine and deserving of this connection and this connection is always in your greatest good!

To connect with Spiritual Source, all we need to do is become aware of our inner divine connection and have the intention to align our energy (vibration). To do so, we turn our attention away from the outside world and bring our awareness to the inner connection of our Soul. We do not need to see or feel our Soul, we just need to recognize that we have an ever-present inner connection that links us to the greater spiritual part of ourselves.

To help with the process of focusing my attention on connecting to my Spirit, I place my attention on my heart chakra center or my solar plexus chakra center. I feel that my heart chakra connects me to all that exists, and my solar plexus chakra communicates to Spiritual Source. When I focus on my heart chakra, I often place my hands over my heart area and focus on feeling a loving connection to everything. I start with loving thoughts toward myself, my husband, my dog, my family and my home, then I move to larger groups such as nature, humanity and Earth. Loving thoughts help me raise my vibration, which puts me into a greater alignment with the higher vibration of Spiritual

Connecting to Spiritual Source

Source. When I focus on communicating to Spiritual Source, I place my hands over my solar plexus chakra (stomach area) and focus on loving thoughts and feelings about what I want to communicate. *We are all unique, so use whatever method intuitively works for you—there isn't a wrong way.*

When doing the following exercises, it helps to find a quiet place to sit, deep breathe, and turn your attention away from your surroundings, bringing your attention inward to focus on your own presence. *Focusing on your own presence is how you go "inward" to your own Soul connection.* When calling upon Source, visualize it as a protective white light surrounding you and focus on loving thoughts that help to raise your vibration to a higher realm, allowing Source to connect more fully with you.

Seeking Protection–

Place your hands above your solar plexus chakra (stomach area). Ask Source: "Please protect me, my home and my loved ones," and whatever else you wish to protect. Visualize yourself and anything else you want to protect surrounded in the white protective light of Spirit. Feel it surrounding you, coming into you and then emanating out of you. Feel Spiritual Source surrounding your home, your loved ones or anything else you desire.

Seeking Healing–

Place your hands above your heart chakra. Your heart chakra is your connection to everything—sickness only comes through the illusion of separation from Spiritual Source. There is no sickness in the collective of Spirit, so focus loving thoughts on connecting to all that exists. Ask: "Source, please bring healing to my body. I ask for your healing white light to flow into my body, healing all my cells and rejuvenating me."

Spiritual Pride

You might visualize a brilliant white light coming through the top of your head and spreading throughout your body. Or you can visualize this light coming into your heart chakra and traveling through your arteries to all parts of your body. This light brings with it high vibrational healing energy while also removing the negative or unhealthy energy. Visualize this negative energy leaving through the bottoms of your feet or leaving on your outward breath. Ask Source to please take it away and recycle this energy.

Seeking Insight–

If you want a place to focus your attention, you can focus on the crown chakra, which is on the top area of your head. Ask: "Source, please give me guidance, answers or wisdom with (any issue that comes to mind)." Please show me paths to get answers or bring them into my mind. I want to know, and I ask for you to please show me."

You can visualize the white light of knowledge coming into your mind or crown chakra delivering the answers you seek. *The answers do not typically appear in the mind suddenly; they usually come into our minds as inspiration or answers at a later time.*

There is no one exact way to connect with Source through our intentions. The words we choose to use, whether we speak them out loud, whisper them or think them quietly in our own heads, is all up to us individually. Just make sure you are comfortable and even excited about your chosen method, because this will lead you to a positive state of mind. Play around with different methods and versions or come up with your own. Your belief in how to make the best connection to Spiritual Source is up for you to decide. This is why a spiritual path is so beautiful—it's as unique as you are!

Trust is in the process. Your intentions are powerful and when you attach positive and loving feelings to them, you share them with Spiritual Source.

A great Awakening has begun. People around the world are opening their eyes to their own spiritual natures. They are beginning to see who they truly are and what they have always been—beings with an eternal past and a glorious future. —Betty Eadie

THE AWAKENED GAY

Nothing is keeping us from awakening to our true spiritual nature and connecting to Spiritual Source but our own ego thoughts. It is, after all, our ego thoughts that we must awaken from to be able to see that we are a divine Spirit having a human experience—an experience that is meant to be loving and enjoyable. By awakening, we begin to see how the ego mind is the source for the judgment, control and hate of this world, and this is exactly the reason why ego thoughts do not exist in spiritual realms. Ego will immerse us in the belief of feeling separate from everything else and also lead us to believe it is what is real, but it is an illusion. Our ego is so convincing that it will even lead us to believe it will go on after death as part of our eternal Spirit, but it does not. Only love and a connection to everything is our reality in the non-physical realms, and because of this, a separate ego cannot exist.

Spiritual Pride

Our ego mind will create its own version of what this world is and what the purpose of our lives are; it's all just part of our unique journey. Some people will become very adamant that their ego ideas about how to live are superior, leading them to go on a mission to make others act the way they do. Yet, no matter how much a person preaches about the right way to live life, people will never agree on one truth or live just one way. In some cultures, there are people in power who are able to force others to fit a certain mold, but they can never change the drive that a person's Soul has instilled within them. Living in a way that forgoes inner desires is out of alignment with Spiritual Source; it takes away the will of our Spirit to freely express itself. This is the reason why ego beliefs will eventually weaken and falter—they are temporary illusions created by the human experience. Once the human experience is over, the individual ego dissipates and our awareness returns to an all knowing and loving state of connectedness.

Individual ego dissipates upon death, but ego beliefs are kept alive and continue on in the human collective—they exist as a form of mental energy that passes from one human to the next. Beliefs are developed; they grow, they change, and they also diminish. The tradition of passing ego beliefs onto the next generation is what trains people to believe some illusions are truth. Beliefs become familiar because of this; people may also believe that their ideas are the sole truth. However, familiarity does not equal truth; it just brings comfort to those who are not able to awaken to see beyond the illusions created by their learned beliefs. There are some beliefs that do resonate as being truthful, but beliefs based on truth will only be found by loving one another and recognizing our connection to everything else. This is the only path to truth because this is how our eternal Spirit exists beyond the illusion of separation.

Spirit does not wish to have a human experience that is degraded, controlled and judged by the human ego ideas of this world. When beliefs become controlling, condemning or negative, they become imbalanced. As a result, a Spirit who wishes to experience individual expression may bring energies into existence that help to balance the imbalanced ego beliefs. These balancing energies will lead to a change in collective beliefs over time through experiences that challenge what people believe to be true. This balancing process can be seen in many aspects of life, but it is especially apparent when Spirit chooses a gay experience. This chosen experience brings those who are close to a gay person to become aware of their judgement and hate toward a lifestyle they were taught was wrong. This leads those who love or care for a gay person to question the condemning beliefs that have been passed onto them, and in many cases, they choose to release the negativity associated with these beliefs.

Ultimately, it's our Spirits decision to have a gay experience, but it's human ego perceptions and decisions that will influence how our lifetimes turn out as a result of being gay. People with condemning beliefs toward gays tend to believe that gays are pushing an agenda to go against the God that they believe in, but the reality is, being gay is a spiritual path chosen by our Spirit.

Our often-unrealized spiritual mission has always been personal; one-on-one, we have been helping the people who are close to us see beyond their closed-minded perceptions. Opening up people's minds and hearts isn't new; gays have been helping others do this for a very long time. Daily we show our friends, families and peers that we are following our inner heart's desire, we are not simply trying to create a counter culture for the purpose of opposing the beliefs of those arounds us. In fact, most of us accept other people's spiritual beliefs; we just don't want to be judged or condemned by others for being who we were born to be.

Those of us who are born gay will feel the inner drive to be gay, but some of us will never understand why we are gay. We may ponder why at some point in our lives, but many of us will not find answers that

Spiritual Pride

make any sense to us. So, instead of soul searching for the reason, we might instead focus on immersing ourselves into gay culture—our alternative culture. Spiritually speaking, gay culture is a beautiful thing. It is based on freedom of expression, which allows our Spirit to express itself more fully, but it can also lead us away from awakening to who we really are.

Gay culture, like many other cultures, leads us to focus outwardly on the thoughts and actions of those around us, while awakening requires us to go within and discover our Spiritual connection. This does not mean that gay culture is something an awakened person must leave behind; instead we can be the person that awakens and adds a compassionate attitude to gay culture. We can also show others why awakening can be beneficial. Gay culture can be both expressive and awakened; in fact, awakening can lead gay culture to be more vibrant, loving, creative and accepting than it is now.

Awakening does not mean withdrawing from life. It means learning to understand life, which allows us to live more fully! When we awaken, we discover who we truly are and what our purpose is. When we awaken, it is life changing! We no longer feel the need to seek validation from those around us because we begin to see the value in ourselves and the lives we are living, regardless of the opinions of others. Awakening leads us to understand why we are gay, and to see judgement from other people for what it is: an illusion based on negative ego beliefs, with no basis in spiritual reality.

As for those of us who have been judged harshly in our lives, awakening allows us to free ourselves from negative ego illusions and take ourselves on a beautiful journey of self-love, self-respect and of living our lives to the fullest. As awakened gays, we recognize our spiritual connection while also having fun and enjoying the entertainment of living in the modern world. We follow our passions and desires, and in doing so, we live authentically. This is in divine order. This is being awakened.

The Awakened Gay

As awakened gay men and women, it is so powerful to know that when we exist in the vibration of love and joy, we are in alignment with the universe, with the Spiritual Source behind all that exists. We know that being gay is not what is wrong with this world; the hate and judgment that we experience from others is what is wrong. The attraction we feel for the same sex and how we choose to express ourselves is in divine order—it is in harmony with Spiritual Source and the universe it works through. With this understanding, we can show through peaceful demonstration that true love exists in gay relationships, and we can be patient with those who have been indoctrinated into limiting beliefs.

But having patience toward those who remain asleep does not mean we become weak in the face of animosity. The awakened stand our ground when we are faced with threats—this is having pride in who we are. Love is always on the right side in this universe and love will continually prevail. No ignorant person or their close-minded beliefs can ever shake our core when we know in our hearts this divine spiritual truth! We remain strong in ignoring judgement, or we choose to take action against those who speak ignorance, but we know better than to take their ignorance to heart.

As awakened gay men and women, we do not need approval or confirmation from others about our beliefs. We know in our hearts what resonates as truth and we allow our truth to empower us. We have the courage to create our own spiritual stories rather than relying on other people's stories or those coming from our ancient past. We realize the concept of spirituality is alive, and it grows with us; it is not something that happened a long time ago and now stays stagnant for millennia. We see spirituality as a sacred and personal union to Spiritual Source, a connection that grows with our awareness. We know when we are presented with universal spiritual truths, we feel a knowing in our hearts—our bodies even tingle with excitement. This is our Soul telling us that what we discovered is in alignment with the universe, and

Spiritual Pride

this is one of the reasons why it feels so good to find our spiritual truth and live by it.

The awakened realize that it is fear and the feeling of being unworthy of God that keep people from having divine spiritual experiences. We realize Spiritual Source does not decide who can connect with it; it is only feeling fearful or unworthy that keeps us from being able to do so. Awakened gay men and women know that we are part of the divine and thus always worthy of connection. We realize there is nothing mysterious about this connection; it's just been made to feel mysterious because truth has historically been shrouded in obscure stories. We choose to live in our current spiritual reality, and because of this, we sense a divine spiritual presence in our everyday lives.

The awakened realize that spirituality is not something we entertain once a week because it is Sunday and we have ignored it the other six days of the week. Instead we see it as part of who we are—as part of our lifestyle. The awakened live a life that balances work and play with getting grounded and centered. We become grounded when we take moments to focus on our connection to Spiritual Source, which brings us back to feeling peace and calm, and we get centered by seeing the bigger picture of what is truly important in our lives. Daily, we see the value in mindful moments or meditating to bring ourselves into alignment with Spiritual Source. We then enjoy the rest of our day with confidence, doing whatever it is that we want to do or being who it is we want to be.

The awakened realize we are a global community; we are all connected to one another and to nature as well. We celebrate the unique personalities that we are born with but we respect our differences and have reverence for the natural world. We understand that life matters and we respect the different cultures and forms of expression around us and across the world. We realize there is no one correct or superior way of living life; we are all on unique and beautiful journeys. Together we form a diverse tapestry of cultures and experiences. We stand united in freedom of expression and we stand up for one another when we see injustices in the world because what hurts one person hurts the Soul of our global community—together we stand united.

The awakened gay is compassionate, intelligent, loving and has moved into a place of being able to understand on a spiritual level who and what we truly are. We understand the difference between the superficial self-love that comes from ego versus true authentic self-love. Self-love coming from ego is based on comparing oneself to others, while authentic self-love means loving ourselves for being who we truly are. True self love comes from expressing ourselves authentically and is enhanced by knowing in our hearts that our gay journey is part of a divine expression.

We are humans and we are Spirit, and we bring peace to our minds through the recognition that we exist as both! Because we are both human and Spirit, we understand that we are in greater alignment with our higher spiritual self when we maintain a high vibration—feeling good about ourselves and maintaining a loving state of mind.

On the other hand, we realize that we exist in a lower vibration and we are less in alignment with our higher spiritual self when we are negative and unloving toward ourselves and others. We realize our physical health suffers when we are negative or low vibrational, so we pay attention to how we feel daily and we make a conscious effort to stay in a positive mindset. To help with this, we balance our stress by taking time to get grounded; we also take the time to work on releasing or balancing our past emotional trauma.

The awakened gay understands the power of manifestation and we keep a positive mental focus on what it is we want for ourselves. We understand we have an ever-present connection to Spiritual Source, and through this positive connection we can experience abundance and well-being. We also understand that like attracts like, and because of this we will attract people and things that match our own vibe. Everything begins with a thought, and we focus our thoughts on working with the infinite intelligence and power of Spiritual Source to help manifest the life we want to live. We also make an effort to get our ego out of the way of receiving the healing energy, creative ideas, intuitive guidance and wisdom that is always coming to us from Spiritual Source.

The awakened gay enjoys traditions and holidays, but we see them as a celebration of life and a coming together with loved ones. We are respectful of the religious ideas that other people hold dear and we join in their prayer with our own form of spiritual connection and loving thoughts. We recognize that others have their own desire for a connection to something divine and we allow them to be on their own path to discovering it. We do not tell them they are wrong in their beliefs or how they should think; we simply love them for who they are. We all have our own truths and comfort levels. We are not better than those who remain asleep; we just have a greater understanding of living life passionately because we realize we are a Spirit having a free will human experience.

"Times are difficult globally; awakening is no longer a luxury or an ideal. It's becoming critical. We don't need to add more depression, more discouragement, or more anger to what's already here. It's becoming essential that we learn how to relate sanely with difficult times. The Earth seems to be beseeching us to connect with joy and discover our innermost essence. This is the best way that we can benefit others." —Pema Chodron

Some things to remember along your spiritual journey:

- Life is simply the journey of your Spirit experiencing being human, so be who it is you want to be. The inner desires you feel are your roadmap to expressing yourself, so follow your heart's desire and immerse yourself in being human; your inner desires will lead you to joy and happiness. Do all the things you want to do, and if you choose, be spiritual about doing it. Your Spirit loves you—you are the human version of itself. The collectives of Spirit that make up Spiritual Source love you for who you are because you are a part of them choosing to have this experience. Love who you are, love what you do and cherish the experience of having a gay lifetime—it is a blessing.

- Your Soul connection to Spiritual Source is alive and well; all you need to do is realize your eternal connection to the source of all that is while being human. Know that you are powerful in dictating your life experience. If you were born into unfortunate circumstances, look for ways to be the creator of your own successful path. If you do not have as much as others, please realize this does not make those with more happier or more fulfilled; it just means they have more things. What will truly make you happy is having a positive perception about yourself and others, not what you have or don't have.

- Forgive yourself for your past mistakes and forgive those who are not awakened and remain under the influence of ego. You have awakened, so let go of the energy of past negative experiences—they no longer serve you.

- ❀ Set boundaries of what is acceptable, and if anyone is incapable of respecting your boundaries, then walk away. You have free will to create your own circles of friends, acquaintances and professional connections. If you were born into an unloving family, you can walk away and create your own family. You are not obligated to be around anyone who does not hold you in the highest regard.

- ❀ Find activities in life that bring you joy and make you feel fulfilled. Positive feelings will put you into spiritual alignment with the universe, and the Spiritual Source behind all that exists. If you want to receive more abundance and wisdom, then let Spiritual Source feel your intention. Feel positively about what it is like to have what you want; Spiritual Source will respond to your intention. Listen to your intuition, you will be mentally inspired and led to synchronicities—events that bring you to what you desire.

- ❀ Always remember, you are loved for being gay by what is eternal and what is true! Be whoever it is you feel in your heart you are and don't let fear stand in your way! Go be where you are cherished and spend your time with those who respect and love you. Go gaily forward and be your fabulous, butch, bear, diva, sassy, witty, lipstick self. Most of all, go be Divine!

About the Author

David Howard, Ph.D, is an author and the owner of Transcendent Lifestyle LLC, which offers guidance in spiritual and metaphysical concepts to help people transform their lives. He received his ministerial doctorate from the University of Sedona, his masters from The University of Metaphysics, and his bachelors in counseling psychology from The Ohio State University. Traditional education by itself did not provide the existential answers David was seeking, so he chose to go to a metaphysical school that taught in depth who and what we really are and why we are having this human experience. Through his metaphysical education and his own exploration, he has discovered that there is a non-physical conscious awareness known as Spirit that we are all ultimately part of and connected to while we are alive. By recognizing this connection and expanding upon it, he has allowed his Spirit to guide him and bring forth the spiritual wisdom that he shares in his books. It is through this wisdom that he has come to the realization that no person needs to conform or change who they are to be on a spiritual path; instead, spirituality should complement who they are and their lifestyle, helping them to find success, happiness and understanding in a hectic and sometimes unexplainable world.

David lives with his husband in Powell, Ohio and enjoys being surrounded by nature, entertaining friends and celebrating life. He is free spirited, fun loving, compassionate to others and passionate about helping people find joy and meaning in their lives.

A note from the author:

Having a connection to Spiritual Source is always in your best interest and it's a loving and beautiful experience! If you need guidance with your spiritual journey or help learning to meditate, I am here for you. You can check out my website **transcendentlifestye.com** for more information or if you are interested in doing exercises to help you grow spiritually, you can check my other book, "The Path to Higher Consciousness: Creating and Healing Our Lives by Awakening to Our Greater Reality." **https://www.amazon.com/author/davidthoward**

Much love to you on your journey,

David Howard, PhD

NOTES

NOTES

www.ingramcontent.com/pod-product-compliance
Lightning Source LLC
LaVergne TN
LVHW051521070426
835507LV00023B/3237